THE

IOUS REMEDIES

AINST

THE

PRECIOUS REMEDIES

AGAINST

SATAN'S DEVICES.

BY THOMAS BROOK.

ABRIDGED BY W. SMELLE, LINCOLNSHIRE, ENGLAND.

Lest Satan should get an advantage of us; for we are not ignorant
of his devices. 2 *Cor.* ii. 11.

EDITED

BY STAUNTON STEVENS BURDOTT,

MINISTER OF THE GOSPEL IN SOUTH CAROLINA.

FIRST AMERICAN EDITION.

NEW HAVEN:

PRINTED FOR THE EDITOR BY NATHAN WHITING.

1832.

CONTENTS.

PREFACE

TO THE FIRST AMERICAN EDITION.

The " Precious Remedies against Satan's Devices,"
by Thomas Brook, is a work of great importance to
every child of God: and if attentively read by them,
it cannot fail to produce on their minds the happiest effects. I conceive it to be one of the most useful books,
aside from the Holy Scriptures, that a Christian can
possess—and one of the best books in the world. It
should be in the possession of every family, and form
an important part of their library. For the importance
of this work is no t confined to the Christian; but it ex-
tends to every individual; and in particular to the youth
of our country. They are drawn imperceptibly by Satan's devices into sin. Not so with the experienced
Christian. The apostle Paul, in his letter to the saints
at Corinth, says, " we are not ignorant of his devices."
But the young are ignorant of his cunning arts to draw
them unto ruin.

It is in this book that the machinations of Satan are
happily brought to view, and the " precious remedies"

1*

pointed out. Therefore to the youth as well as to the aged this work must be valuable.

And in presenting the present edition to the christian public, it is with the earnest desire, that it may prove a great blessing to the youth of our land, and to the tempted followers of the b essed Jesus. The remedies are indeed precious. And they should be so regarded by every Christian.

And may God grant that this effort of his servant, (who is now, I trust, in heaven,) to advance his kingdom, prove a precious remedy to those who are exposed to the devices of him who "goeth about as a roaring lion, seeking whom he may devour." That God may be glorified in the happy life, triumphant death, and consummate bliss of poor sinners saved by grace, is the prayer of the

EDITOR.

LONG TOWN, S. C., June, 1832.

PREFACE

TO THE ENGLISH EDITION.

———

THE knowledge of men and things may be of some use in the affairs of life; but the knowledge of the human heart, and the Devices of Satan exceedeth all. Whosoever is possessed of so valuable a branch of knowledge, is thereby enabled to judge rightly of himself, and to find out the various wiles of the devil practised against his own soul, and the souls of others. Lest Satan should get an advantage of us: i. e. overreach us.

The comparison is taken from a greedy merchant, that seeketh and taketh all opportunities to beguile and deceive others. Satan is this greedy merchant, that seeketh to devour the souls of men.

We are not ignorant of Satan's devices, plots, machinations, and stratagems, which he practices to waylay the souls of men. Satan hath snares for the wise and snares for the simple; snares for hypocrites and snares for the upright; snares for generous souls and snares for timorous souls; snares for the rich and snares for the poor; and snares for the aged, and snares for the youth.

Oh! what depths of Satan and the human heart may yet be discovered by a diligent attendance to the work-

ings of the mind ! For, while I speak of the devices of Satan, I would not have any to suppose that I exempt the
human heart from being a principal agent in these devices of Satan. Notwithstanding the grace of God pro-
duceth in the heart an hatred of all sin, and a love to
truth, so that the soul may say, though there be no one
sin in me absolutely routed, or conquered as it should,
yet truly every sin is hateful, and loathed by me ; and though
I do not obey any one commandment of God as I ought,
and as I would do, yet (the pious soul can say that) every
word of God is good, and every commandment is precious,
and what I daily prize; therefore though I cannot strict-
ly fulfil all the righteous will and commandments of my
God, there are none but what I would most gladly keep,
and hate in me that which wars against my soul for delighting in the law with my inward man. Satan and the human
heart are mighty in abilities to deceive. Satan has
long studied the heart of man, and is master of every
secret avenue; and he well knows that there is no power upon earth that is so well qualified, and that would
prove so faithful to his devices, as the human heart;
therefore he will not with a little feeble effort, be persuaded
to relinquish his possession of the heart: yea, he is a
strong man, armed, &c., and it requireth the strength of
the strongest, even the Almighty, to bind Satan, and cast
him out of the heart of man ; nevertheless, any thing
that tendeth to a discovery of so grand and so secret an
enemy, ought to be esteemed precious. Though the
discovery may be attended with some difficulty, yet the
end and conquest will repay with unspeakable joy.

I am free to confess, that I never read or saw any
work, next to the blessed book, the bible, that appears

(to me, at least,) so complete a pursuit and detection of Satan and the human heart, as the Precious Remedies against Satan's Devices. The title is truly in the work, and the work is the glory of the title. I have abridged some parts, where I judged the subject had been stated with advantage in some other part of the work; I have also introduced this work with a few introductory propositions from the conclusion of the author; and I have taken the liberty to reduce it from the form of a sermon, which it originally bore, to that of chapters, and to each chapter appointed six remedies; I have also applied a portion of scripture to each chapter and remedy, that the several devices and remedies might be easily read and distinguished; hoping herein to assist the reader, to take the devil in his own craftiness, to save the souls of men, and to cast some light on more than two hundred texts of scripture; all which is possible to him under whose care and influence this humble attempt was begun, and unto whose glory may it tend forever. Amen, and Amen.

W. SMELLE,

TO THE READER.

Solomon bids us buy the truth, but doth not tell us what it must cost; because we must get it though it be never so dear; we must love it, shining and scorching: every part of truth is precious as the filings of gold; we must live and die with it, as Ruth said to Naomi, "Whither thou goest I will go, and where thou lodgest I will lodge," &c., for nothing shall part the soul and truth. A man may sell his house and lands lawfully, but truth is a jewel that exceeds all price, and must not be sold, for it is our heritage. Psal. cxix. 111. 'Tis a legacy that our forefathers have bought with their blood. If thou, Reader, pleasest to read this work, and receive counsel from me, thou must first know, that every man cannot be excellent that yet may be useful. An iron key may unlock the door of a golden treasure; yea, iron can do some things that gold cannot.

Secondly, remember that 'tis not hasty reading, but serious meditating upon holy and heavenly truths, that makes them prove sweet and profitable to the soul. 'Tis not the bee's touching the flower that gathers honey, but her abiding for a time upon it that draws out the sweet: therefore it is not he that reads most, nor he that talks most, but he that meditates most, that will prove the choicest and strongest Christian. If thou knowest these things, happy and blessed art thou if thou doest them.

" Not every one that saith, Lord. Lord, shall enter into the kingdom of heaven, but he that doeth the will of my Father that is in heaven." Matt. vii. 21.

Reader, if it be not strongly impressed upon thy mind to practice what thou readest, to what purpose dost thou read? Thy knowledge will be that rod that will eternally lash thee, that scorpion that will for ever bite thee, and that worm that will everlastingly gnaw thee. Seneca saith I like not such persons who are always about to live but never begin. God loves the runner, not the questioner, saith Luther. When Demosthenes was asked what was the first part of an orator, what the second, and what the third? he answered, action. If any should inquire what is the first, the second, and the third part of a Christian? I will answer, action.

I pray and desire that thou mayest find as much sweetness, &c. in reading this Treatise, as I have found in the writing of it. I recommend thee to God and to the word of his grace, which is able to build thee up, and to give thee an inheritance among them which are sanctified. And rest,

Reader,

Thy soul's servant in every office of the gospel,

THOMAS BROOK.

INTRODUCTION.

THAT Satan hath a great hand in sin cannot be
denied ; yet ought we to be careful that we do not
lay all the blame of our sins, and compliance with
temptations, upon Satan, and so father that upon him
which should, in justice, be charged upon our own
evil hearts. Sin and evading came into the world together. The whole frame of man is out of order :
the understanding is darkness ; the will is cross and
rebellious ; the affections are crooked ; the conscience
corrupted ; the tongue poisoned ; and the heart
evil, only evil, and that continually. Satan hath
only a persuading, not an enforcing might ; he can
tempt, but cannot conquer without our hearts : yet
Satan tempted our first parents to rebellion, moved
David to number Israel, put Peter upon rebuking
Christ, entered into the heart of Judas to persuade
him to betray his Lord and Master, and filled the
heart of Ananias, and Sapphira his wife, to lie to the
Holy Ghost. Such, therefore, is Satan's malice
against God, and his envy against men, that he will
resolutely have a hand in all Sin, one way or other.

Satan must obtain permission of God before he
can prevail against us. Job. ii. 6. The Lord said
unto Satan, behold, he is in thine hand. The devil

2

has malice sufficient to devour, but hath not power
so much as to touch the least and the weakest of
God's children, without a commission. How long
did he try to destroy Job, but in vain? What attempts did he make to ruin Peter and his companions, and desired to have them, that he might sift
them as wheat? But Jesus prayed for them. So
Satan seeks to overthrow you, as he did Saul, Ahab,
and others. But what a soul-supporting consolation and cordial is the consideration, that the greatest, subtlest, and the most daring enemy of the saints,
cannot hurt or harm them without special leave from
him who is their sweetest Saviour, their dearest husband, and their choicest friend. Ambrose represents the devil as boasting over Jesus Christ, in Judas: he is not thine, Lord Jesus, he is mine: his
heart beats for me; he eats with thee, but is fed by
me; he takes bread from thee, but money from me;
he drinks wine with thee, but sells thy blood to me.

As Satan must obtain permission from God, so
must he also gain the consent of our hearts before he
can prevail. Acts. v. 3. Why hath Satan filled thine
heart to lie? Satan can never undo a man without
himself; but a man may easily undo himself without
Satan: he can only present the glory of the world,
but cannot force us to fall down and worship him.
When he tempts, we must assent; when he makes
offers, we must accept; when he commands, we
must obey; and when he threatens, we must fear, or

he will labor in vain. Peter expostulates the case with Ananias, Why hast thou given Satan such an advantage over thee, to fill thy heart with infidelity, hypocrisy, and obstinate audacity, to lie to the Holy Ghost? As if he had said, Ananias, Satan could never have done this in thee, (which will forever undo thee,) unless thou hadst granted him access to thine heart. If, when a temptation comes, a man cries out, and saith, Ah! Lord, here is a strong temptation that would force me, and that would devour my soul. I have of myself no strength to withstand. Oh! help, help thou me ; for thy Son's sake, for thy promise sake, and for my soul's sake : then it is not the soul that consents, but Satan that has forced.

PRECIOUS REMEDIES

SATAN'S DEVICES.

CHAP. I.

SATAN'S FIRST DEVICE TO DRAW THE SOUL TO SIN, IS TO REPRESENT THE BAIT AND HIDE THE HOOK.

GENESIS iii. 5.
Ye shall be as Gods, &c.

OH! saith Satan, fear not. Ye shall not surely die: for the Lord doth know, that in the day ye eat thereof then your eyes shall be opened, and ye shall be as gods, knowing good and evil. Here is the bait, the sweet, the pleasure, and the profit. Oh! but the hook, the shame, the wrath, and the loss that would inevitably attend the compliance, he carefully hides. There is an opening of the eyes of the mind to contemplation and joy, and there is an opening of the eyes of the body to shame and confusion: Satan promiseth them the former, and intendeth the last; and so deceives them, giving them an apple in exchange for Paradise.

2*

The Precious Remedies against this device of Satan are these:

First. To keep at the greatest distance from sin.

1 THESSALONIANS v. 22.
Abstain from all appearance of Evil.

ANSELM used to say, that if he should see the shame of sin on the one hand, and the pains of hell on the other, and must of necessity choose one, he would rather be thrust into hell without sin, than go into heaven with sin. 'Tis our wisest and safest course to stand at the furthest distance from sin, and to fly from all appearance of evil. It is surely the best method to prevent any person from falling into the pit, to keep at the greatest distance from it. He that will be so bold as to play upon the brink of the pit, may find, by woeful experience, that it is a righteous thing with God that he should fall into the snare. Joseph kept himself at a proper distance from sin, and from attempting to play with the golden bait, though continually urged by his mistress; yet he retires, and abstains from all appearance of evil, with a " how can I do this great wickedness, and sin against God?" David boldly draws nigh, and sports with the bait; but, at last, he is snared and taken, and laments the folly of it all his days.

The second Remedy is, humbly to consider that sin is a plague.

1 KINGS viii. 38.
The plague of his own heart.

Sin is a plague, yea, the greatest and most infectious plague in all the world; yet, alas! how few are there that tremble at it? As soon as one sin had seized upon Adam's heart, all sin entered into his soul, and overspread it. And how hath Adam's one sin spread over all mankind? Rom. v. 12. Ah! how doth the father's sin infect the child: the husband's infect the wife; the master's, the servant? Yes, the sin that is in one man's heart is able to infect a whole world. The Italian, who first made his enemy deny God, to save his life, did afterwards stab him, and then boasted, that he had at once murdered both soul and body, declares the perfect malignity of sin. 'Twas a good saying of a heathen, that if there were no God to punish him, no devil to torment him, no hell to burn him, no man to see him, yet would he not sin, for the ugliness and filthiness of sin, and for the grief of his own conscience—"I will not buy repentance so dear: I am not so ill a merchant as to sell eternals for temporals." *Demosthenes.*

The third Remedy is, carefully to consider that sin is but a bitter-sweet.

Job xx. 12, 13, 14.

Though wickedness be sweet in the mouth, it is the gall of asps within.

The seeming sweetness that is in sin will quickly vanish, and lasting shame, sorrow, horror, and terror will come in the room thereof. Adam's apple was a bitter-sweet; Esau's mess was a bitter-sweet; the Israelites' quails were a bitter-sweet; and Adonijah's kingly sweets proved a bitter-sweet unto him: for after the feast comes the reckoning. When the asp stings a man, it doth at first tickle him so as to make him laugh, till the poison, by little and little, gets to his heart; then it pains him more than ever it could delight him before : so doth sin —it may please a little at first, but it will pain the soul with a witness at last; yea, if there were the least real sweet or delight in sin, there could be no perfect hell, where men must be eternally tormented with their sins. Forbidden profits and pleasures are most pleasing to vain men, who count madness mirth. Many long to be meddling with the murdering morsels of sin, which nourish not, but rent and consume the belly and the soul that receive them. Many eat that on earth which they are forced to digest in hell.

The fourth Remedy is, solemnly to consider that sin will bring upon us infinite losses.

MARK viii. 36, 37.
Gain the world and lose the soul.

Sin will usher in the loss of the Divine favor that is better than life; the loss of that joy which is unspeakable and full of glory; the loss of that peace that passeth all understanding; the loss of those divine influences by which the soul hath been refreshed, quickened, raised, strengthened, and gloriously led to triumph in the divine light: and the loss of many outward, desirable mercies, which otherwise the soul might have enjoyed.

That was a sound and savory reply of an English captain, at the loss of Calais, who, when a proud Frenchman scornfully demanded, "When will you fetch Calais again?" replied, "When your sins shall weigh down ours."

Ah! England, England, my constant prayer for thee is, that thou mayest not sin away thy mercies into their hands, that cannot call mercy, mercy, and that would joy in nothing more than to see thy sorrow and misery, and to see that hand to make thee naked which hath long clothed thee with much glory and mercy.

The fifth Remedy is, seriously to consider that sin is very deceitful and hardening.

HEBREWS iii. 13.
Hardened through the deceitfulness of sin.

Sin is the greatest deceiver in the world; it will kiss the soul, and pretend fair to us to our face, but will betray the soul forever: it will, with Delilah, smile upon us, that it may betray us into the hands of the devil, as she did Sampson into the hands of the Philistines. Sin gave Satan his power over us; and he lays claim to us as those who wear his badge and mark. Sin is a very bewitching thing upon the human heart, that the soul calls good, evil; and evil, good; bitter, sweet; and sweet, bitter; light, darkness; and darkness, light; and the soul bewitched with sin, will stand out against God, even unto death. Let the Almighty strike and wound, even unto the bone, the soul cares not, nor fears not: see Pharoah, Balaam, and Judas. There is an herb in Sardis, that would make a man lye laughing on his bed when he was deadly sick; such is the operation of sin. Prov. v. 22, 23.

The sixth Remedy is, attentively to consider that there is neither rest nor peace in sin.

ISAIAH lvii. 20, 21.
Like the troubled sea.

For the curse, the wrath, the hatred, and indignation of God doth always attend sin and sinners.

The curse of God haunts the sinner (as it were a fury) in all his ways: in the city it attends him, in the country it hovers over him; coming in it accompanies him, going forth it follows him; in travel it is his comrade; it fills his store with strife, and mingles the wrath of God with his sweetest morsels; it is a moth in his wardrobe, murrain among his cattle, mildew in his field, rot among his sheep, and oftentimes makes the fruit of his loins the greatest vexation and confusion of his life. There is no solid joy nor lasting peace to a sinner in his sins, for the sword of divine vengeance doth every moment hang over his head. Syrens sing wonderfully curious while they live, but roar most dreadfully horrible when they die; so must the ungodly sinner. Deut. xxviii. 15. to the end. Levit. xxvi. 14. to the end.

CHAP. II.

THE SECOND DEVICE OF SATAN IS TO PAINT SIN WITH VIRTUE'S COLORS.

1 KINGS xxii. 22.
A lying spirit.

SATAN knows, that if he should present sin in its own nature and dress, the soul would rather fly from it than yield to it ; therefore he presents sin unto us, not in its own proper colors, but painted and disguised ; gilded over with names and shew of virtue, that we may be more easily overcome by it, and so take the greater pleasure in committing of it. Pride he presents to the soul under the name and notion of neatness and cleanliness in life. Covetousness, (which the apostle condemns for idolatry,) Satan points out to be good husbandry in a family. Drunkenness which is an open sin, Satan pleads for, and persuades the soul that it is but cheerfulness and good fellowship. Riotousness, Satan presents under the fair name and notion of liberty and liberality to mankind : and wantonness he represents only as a trick of youth.

The precious Remedies against this device are these :

First. To consider that sin is nevertheless sin, and vile, though painted.

JEREMIAH iv. 30.
Though thou rentest thy face with painting, in vain shalt thou make thyself fair.

Surely sin cannot be one degree the less filthy, vile, and abominable, by its being colored and varnished with virtue's colors. A poisonous pill is no less poisonous though it is gilded over with gold ; a wolf is no less a wolf, although he hath put on a sheep's skin ; and the devil is nevertheless a devil, and an adversary to souls, though he may sometimes appear like an angel of light: so sin is no less sin, and abominable unto the pious soul, in crimson, and decked with ornaments of gold, than when it is in rags : and thus the evils of the heart are to be loathed and watched, though they may appear to be at peace with us.

The second Remedy is, carefully to consider, that the more sin is painted and colored with virtue, it is the more dangerous to souls.

2 SAMUEL xx. 9. 10.
Art thou in health my brother ? So he smote him.

That the more sin is varnished, and appears as a friend to virtue, the more ruinous it is to the souls of men ; that while it asketh after our health and peace
3

as a brother, and takes us by the beard with the right
hand, to kiss, it stabs us with the sword in the left,
as Joab did Amasa. This is so notoriously known,
that I need but name it. The most dangerous vermin are too often to be found under the fairest and
sweetest flower; the neatest glove is often drawn
upon the foulest hand; and the richest robes are often put upon the filthiest bodies: so are the fairest
and sweetest names put upon the greatest and the
most horrible vices and errors that are in the world.
Ah! that we had not too many sad proofs of this
among us at this day.

The third Remedy is, to look on sin with proper
eyes.

GENESIS iii. 7.

Their eyes were open and they knew that they were
naked.

To view sin with open eyes, or with such eyes as
within very little time we shall see it before the throne
of God. Ah! souls, when you shall lie upon a dying bed, and stand before a judgment seat, sin will
be unmasked, and its dress and robes shall then be
all taken off, and then it will appear more vile, filthy,
and terrible than hell itself. Oh! my soul, the
shame, the pain, the gall, and alarming consternation
to our first parents, when they saw sin undressed
and naked! So the sinner at death or at the bar of

God, will find, to his eternal astonishment, sin is a monster, in whatsoever dress it hath appeared to men. Conscience will work at last: though for the present you may feel no fit of pain or accusation, sin will be bitterness in the end. Satan deals with men now as the panther doth with the beasts; he hides his deformed head until the sweet scent hath drawn them into danger: so Satan is a parasite until we sin, then he turns a tyrant.

The fourth Remedy is, seriously to consider, that even those very sins that Satan painteth as virtues, require infinite love and power to redeem us from them.

1 TIMOTHY iii. 16.

Great is the mystery of godliness.

Yes, those very sins that Satan paints and puts new names and colors upon, cost the best love, the noblest love, the heart-love of the Lord Jesus. That Christ should come from the eternal bosom of his father to a region of sorrow and death; that God should be manifest in the flesh; the Creator made a creature; that the Eternal, who was clothed with infinite glory, should be wrapped with rags of flesh; that he who filled heaven and earth with his brightness should be laid in a manger; that the power of God should fly from weak man; [the God of Israel went into Egypt;] that the God of the law should be subject to the law; that he who binds Satan in chains should be tempted by the devil; that he who is the judge of all flesh should be judged and condemned; that the God of life should be put to death; that he who hath the keys of hell and death should lie imprisoned in the grave, to save guilty men from sin and death eternal, was infinite love indeed!

The fifth Remedy is, solemnly to consider, that freedom from sin cost an infinite price.

1 PETER i. 19.
Precious blood of Christ.

Every sin is costly to the Redeemer. Yea, sins colored with virtue cost the best blood, the noblest blood, the heart's-blood of Jesus Christ. Ah! my soul, to see that face which was fairer than the sons of men, spit on; that 'mouth and tongue, which spake as never man spake, accused of blasphemy; those hands and feet, that swayed the sceptre of heaven, and shined as fine brass, nailed to the cross for my sins!

After Julius Cæsar was murdered, Antonius brought forth his coat, all bloody and cut, and laid it before the people, saying, " Look, here you have your Emperor's coat, thus bloody and torn ;" whereupon all the people were presently in an uproar, and

run and slew and burnt the murderers. So let my
soul arise and slay those sins, the monstrous murderers of my Lord.

When Dionysius, in Egypt, heard the noise, and
saw the eclipse of the sun at the time of Christ's sufferings he cried out, "Either the God of nature suffers, or the world will be dissolved."

The sixth Remedy is, seriously to consider, that
the soul will never be able to endure the weight of
the least sin.

NUMBERS xxxii. 23.

Be sure your sin will find you out.

The soul is never able to abide the guilt and
weight of the least sin, when God shall set it home
upon the mind: the least sin will press and sink the
stoutest sinner as low as hell. What so little, base,
and vile among creatures as lice? Yet God so plagued the stout-hearted Pharoah; yea, and all Egypt
fainted under them, and the greatest men were forced to cry out, "this is the finger of God." Just so,
when God shall cast the sword into the hand of a
little sin, and arm it against the soul of man, the
stoutest sinner shall faint and fall before it. One
drop of an evil conscience will swallow up the
whole sea of worldly joy.—Mr. Perkins makes

3*

mention of a good, but very poor man, who, being
ready to starve, stole a lamb, and being about to
eat it with his family, and (as his manner was before meat) to crave a blessing upon it, he durst
not do it, but fell into a great perplexity of soul, and
went and acknowledged his fault to the owner, and
promised payment.

CHAP. III.

THE THIRD DEVICE OF SATAN TO DRAW THE SOUL,
TO SIN, IS TO REPRESENT GOD AS ONE MADE UP
ALL OF MERCY.

GENESIS iii. 4.
Ye shall not surely die.

OH! saith Satan, though God hath said that ye
shall die, he doth not so intend; he is too great and
merciful to punish you, for so small a fault as this.
You need not make so great a matter of sin. Do
not be so fearful of sinning, nor so unwilling to this:
is it not a little one? And God is a God of mercy,
a God full of mercy, a God that delights in mercy, a
God that is ready to shew mercy, a God never weary of exercising mercy, and a God that is more prone
to pardon sin in his people, than to punish them for
it; therefore he will not take any advantage of you:
why then should you be so thoughtful about sin?
And, besides all this, God is become more merciful
and kind through his Son Jesus Christ; there is
nothing now for you to fear; Christ died for all sinners, and you are but a sinner.

———

The precious Remedies against this device of Satan are these :.

First. To consider, that to be given up of God to our own wills is the greatest hell upon earth.

ROMANS i. 28.

God gave them over to a reprobate mind.

That is the sorest judgment in the world to be left to sin, upon any pretence whatever. Oh! unhappy man, when God leaveth thee to thyself, to thy free will, and doth not resist thee in thy choice, and in thy sins. Wo, wo to him at whose sins God doth wink. When the Lord suffers the way to sin and hell to be smooth and pleasant unto the heart, it is an awful token that he doth not intend good unto that man: for my own part, I pray as much to be kept from my sinful self, and my free will, as I do from Satan and hell; for a soul given up to its own invention and sin, is a soul ripe for hell. "Ephraim is joined to idols; let him alone." Hosea iv. 17. Psal. lxxxi. 12.—Ah! Lord! this mercy I humbly beg, that whatever thou shalt see good to deliver me up to, thou wilt not give me up to the ways of my own heart: shouldest thou give me up to be afflicted, or tempted, or reproached, &c. I will say, *it is the Lord.* 2 Sam. xv. 26. Only deliver me from that evil man, myself.

The second Remedy is, seriously to consider, that God is as just as he is merciful.

2 PETER ii. 4.
For if God spared not the angels.

Against this artful device of Satan let us consider, that though the scriptures represent the mercy of God in beautiful and striking colors, yet they also speak him to be a just and holy God, and will by no means clear the guilty. The casting of the angels out of heaven, and binding them in chains of darkness till the judgment of the great day; the turning of Adam out of Paradise : the drowning of the old world ; the raining down from heaven of fire and brimstone upon Sodom and Gomorrah; but above all, witness the pouring forth of his wrath upon his own only beloved Son, when he bare our sins, and cried, "My God, My God, why hast thou forsaken me ?" Oh ! Christian, it was all for thee and for me that Jesus was forsaken of his Father, that he might know how to comfort thee under the hidings of thy Father's countenance.

The third Remedy is, Humbly to consider that sins against mercy are attended with the heaviest judgments from God.

HEBREWS ii. 3.
How shall we escape ?

Mercy is Alpha, Justice is Omega. David, speaking of these attributes, placed Mercy in the front, and Justice in the rearward, saying, "My song shall be of mercy and judgment." But sins against mercy will bring down the greatest and sorest judgments upon the heads and hearts of men that can be inflicted by the Lord upon the rebel. Let us consider this in the Israelites ; the Lord loved, them, and chose them to be his people before all people, and that when they were in their blood : he multiplied them, not by means, but by miracles ; and from seventy souls they grew, in a few years, to six hundred thousand ; the more they were oppressed, the more they prospered. But they abused the mercy of the Lord, and soon became the objects of his severest wrath. As I know not the man that can reckon up their mercies, so I know not the man that can sum up their miseries ; for God was turned against them.

The fourth Remedy is, diligently to consider, that God's special mercy is over the righteous.

ISAIAH liv. 8.
With everlasting kindness will I have mercy on thee.

Let us remember, that though God's general mercy be over all his works, yet his special mercy is only to those that love him, and are the called according to his purpose. Exod. xxxiv. 67. Psal. xxv. 10; xxxiii, 18; and ciii. 11, 17. When Satan, therefore, tempts to draw thee to sin, by presenting God as a God made up all of mercy, oh! then reply, that though it be true that God's general mercy extendeth to all his works, yet his loving kindness is confined to them that fear him, to them that love him and keep his commandments; therefore, if ever I taste his mercy in a saving sense to my soul, it must be through his infinite goodness and grace in Jesus Christ, or else I must eternally perish in everlasting misery, notwithstanding all the mercy of God in natural life.

The fifth Remedy is, solemnly to consider, that all those that do taste and see that God is gracious unto them, find that the greatest victory over sin is drawn from the mercies of God.

2 CORINTHIANS xiii. 8.
We can do nothing against the truth.

Yea, the souls that were once glorious on earth, and are now triumphing in heaven, did all look upon the mercy of God as the most powerful argument to preserve them from sin. Psal. xxvi. 3, 4, 5. So Joseph strengthens himself against sin: he kept his eyes fixed upon mercy, and therefore sin could not enter. There can be nothing in the world that renders a man more unlike a child of God, and more like to the devil, than to argue from mercy to sinful liberty; from divine goodness to licentiousness: this is Satan's logic, and wheresoever you find this you may write, this man's soul is lost. A man may as well say that the sea burns him, and the fire makes him cool, as to say that the grace and mercy of God encourages him to sin. Rom. vi. 1, 2. And if these mercies will not do these glorious things for us, you may write us void of all good, Christless and hopeless forever.

The sixth Remedy is, seriously to reflect upon that strict account sinners must give of all the mercies they have enjoyed.

LUKE xvi. 25.
Son, remember in thy life-time, &c.

Ah! did men but dwell more upon the mercies they have received, and the account that they must ere long give of them, they would cry out, in anguish of soul, "Oh! that our mercies had been fewer, that our account might have been easier, and our torment and misery, for our abuse of those infinite mercies, not greater than we are able to bear."

Philip the third of Spain, whose life was free from gross evils, professed, that he would rather lose all his kingdom than offend God willingly; yet at his death cried out "Oh! would to God I had never reigned! Oh! that those years I have spent in my

kingdom I had lived a solitary life in the wilderness!
Oh, that I had lived a solitary life with God; how
much more securely should I now die! What doth
all my glory profit me? but only causeth me so
much the more torment of soul in my death."

The sleeping of vengeance causeth the overflow-
ing of sin, and the overflowings of sin cause the
awakening of vengeance: abused mercy will certainly turn into fury.

4

CHAP. IV.

THE FOURTH DEVICE OF SATAN IS, TO REPRESENT SIN AS A LITTLE THING.

GENESIS xix. 20.

It is but a little one; and my soul shall live.

BY extenuating and lessening sin, Satan gets an advantage over us; and when we are ignorant of his devices, we pass on until we are snared and taken. Ah! saith Satan, 'tis but a little pride, a little worldliness, a little cheerful company; It is a poor heart that never rejoices; and at most it can be but a very little sin, and what may be committed without danger, when compared with others who defile themselves with all manner of sin and uncleanness daily, wherein I can mean no harm; and when I do sit and chat, and even sip with the drunkard, I am not like him that sits drinking himself drunk, swearing, and uttering all manner of lewdness. Thus we not only stand upon comparison, but upon disparison: I am not as this publican.

———

The precious Remedies against this device of Satan are these:

First. To consider, that although sins be not all equally heinous, yet the least deserves eternal death.

JAMES i. 15.

Lust conceived, bringeth forth sin: sin finished, bringeth forth death.

Let us reflect, that those sins which we are apt to account small, have brought upon men the greatest wrath of God: as the eating of the forbidden fruit; the gathering of sticks on the Sabbath; and the touching of the ark. Oh! the dreadful wrath that little sins have brought down from heaven upon men? The least is contrary to the law of God, the nature of God, the being, and the glory of God, and therefore it is often punished severely by the Lord.

And do we not see and hear, almost daily, the vengeance of the Almighty falling on the heads of some one sinner or other? Surely, if we are not utterly left of God, and blinded by Satan, we cannot but know these things. Oh! therefore, when Satan saith 'tis but a little one, do you say, " Oh! but those sins that thou callest little are such that will cause the anger of God forever." Cæsar was stabbed with a bodkin; Pope Adrian was choaked with a gnat; King Lysimachus stopped to drink a draught of water, and lost his kingdom for it: so the least sin unpardoned will ruin the soul forever.

The second Remedy is, carefully to consider, that the giving way to less sins generally makes a way for greater.

2 SAMUEL xii. 9.

Wherefore hast thou despised the commandment of the Lord?

If we commit one sin to avoid another, it is just that we should avoid neither ; for he that to avoid a greater sin will yield to a lesser, ten thousand to one but God, in justice, will leave his soul to fall into the greater. David first gave way to the wandering of his eyes, and this led him to a train of foul sins that caused God to break his bones, and to leave his soul in darkness. Jacob, Peter, and other saints, have found this true by woful experience, that the yielding to a little sin hath been the ushering in of a greater. Ah ! how many have in our days fallen, first to have low thoughts of the scriptures and ordinances, and then to slight the scriptures and ordinances, counting them a nose of wax, and so at last to advance and lift up themselves and their Christ-dishonoring and soul-damning opinions above the scriptures and ordinances ! When a man begins to sin he knows not where or when he must stop.

The third Remedy is, seriously to consider, that the children of God have chose to suffer the worst of torments here, rather than give way to the least sin.

DANIEL iii. 30.

If it be so, our God is able to deliver; but if not, we will not serve thy gods.

Some saints have chosen to suffer the worst of torments rather than they would commit the least sin. (i. e. such as the world accounts least.) Behold Daniel and his companions, that would rather choose to burn, and be cast to lions, than they would bow to the image that Nebuchadnezzar had set up. When this is the case with a man, that he must either fall into sin or be cast into the fiery furnace, Satan bids him sin to save himself: it is but a little thing to bow the knee to an image; but true grace saith, try the furnace, thy God is able to deliver: but if not, it is far better to burn for not sinning, than that God and conscience should raise a hell in thy bosom for sin. Thus we must choose rather to suffer the worst of punishments that men and devils can invent and inflict, than commit the least sin whereby God should be dishonored, conscience and religion wounded, and our souls endangered.

The fourth Remedy is, solemnly to consider, that there is more evil in the least sin than in the greatest affliction.

4*

LAMENTATIONS iii. 39.
Wherefore doth a living man complain?

That there is a greater evil in the least sin than in the greatest affliction, appears as clear as the sun at noon-day, if we do but reflect upon the severe dealing of God the Father with the infinite person of his beloved Son, (and that in the room and place of sinners,) who poured out the vials of his fiercest wrath upon him, yea, and that for the least sin as well as the greatest. *The wages of sin is death;* of sin indefinitely, whether great or small. Oh! brethren, how should this make us tremble, as much at the least spark of lust as at hell itself! considering, that God the Father would not spare his own Son, his bosom Son, yea, his eternal Son, no, not for the least sin, but would have him drink the dregs of his wrath to make satisfaction for sin through his blood. Oh! my soul, there is therefore no little sin, because there is no little God to sin against.

The fifth Remedy is, seriously to consider, that God will proportion his judgments to the nature of the offence.

MATTHEW xxv. 26.
Thou wicked and slothful servant.

This man's sins lay in his slothfulness, in not doing the good he might, and in entertaining wrong thoughts of God, and bringing false charges against his providence and grace, supposing and complaining of them as unequally distributed amon g men. How many of this cast are there in the world at this day? God will suit men's punishments to their sins; the greatest sins shall be attended with the greatest punishments, and the lesser, (so called by men,) with lesser judgments. Alas ! what a poor comfort will this be to thee when thou comest to die, to consider, in thy departing moments, that thou shalt not be equally tormented with other sinners, and yet knowest that thou must be shut out forever from the glorious presence of God, of Christ, of angels, and of saints, and from those great and good things of eternal life, that are so many that they exceed all number, so great that they exceed all measure, and so precious that they exceed every estimation?

The sixth Remedy is carefully to consider, that nothing but the truth can keep us from sin.

2 TIMOTHY i. 13.
Hold fast sound words.

Truth is more precious than gold or rubies ; and all things that thou canst desire are not to be compared to her. Truth is that heavenly glass wherein we may see the lustre and glory of divine wisdom, power, greatness, love, and mercy : in this glass you may behold the face of Christ, the riches of Christ, the heart of Christ, beating sweetly towards your souls. Oh! let our souls cleave to the truth as a guide to lead us, a staff to uphold us, a cordial to strengthen, and a balm to heal all our wounds. Is not truth our right eye, without which we cannot behold Jesus; our right hand, without which we can do nothing for Christ; and our right foot, without which we cannot walk with God? The crown is the top of royalties; so is truth; let no man take thy crown. "Hold fast the faithful word." Titus. i. 9.

CHAP. V.

THE FIFTH DEVICE OF SATAN TO DRAW THE SOUL
TO SIN, IS BY REPRESENTING [TO MEN] THE SINS
OF THE GREATEST SAINTS, AND HIDING THEIR RE-
PENTANCE.

ECCLESIASTES vii. 20.
Not a just man upon earth.

YEA, saith Satan, dost thou not know that Noah
was a just man, and perfect in his generation? " And
Noah walked with God." Yet Noah was guilty of
drunkenness. Lot was a righteous man, and "Lot's
righteous soul was vexed from day to day with the
filthy conversation of the wicked;" yet even he committed incest with his daughters. Abraham and
Isaac were good men, yet both denied their wives.
Jacob was a man of piety, but he was guilty of both
deceit and lies. David was a man after God's own
heart, yet he committed adultery, and shed innocent
blood. In short, Satan artfully states the pride of
Hezekiah, the impatience of Job, the blasphemy of
Peter, &c. as encouragements to the soul to sin without despair; but carefully hideth from the soul the
tears, the sighs, the groans, the meltings, the hum-
blings, and the repentings of these pious men.

The precious Remedies against this device of Satan are these:

First.   Faithfully to remember, that the Spirit of God hath been as careful in describing the repentance of these saints as he was particular in noticing their sins.

JOB xlii. 6.

I abhor myself, and repent in dust and ashes.

'Tis true, O Satan, that saints do fall fearfully when left to themselves; but by repentance they all rise sweetly, and become ensamples for us; and by the Spirit of the Lord they are set forth as beacons, to direct our way. 'Tis true, Job curses the day of his birth; but behold him in the text. Peter falls dreadfully; but see his repentance; Christ looks upon him and melts him into tears. Clement notes, that Peter so repented that all his life after, every night when he heard the cock crow, he would fall upon his knees, and weeping bitterly would crave pardon for this sin. Ah! souls, you can easily sin with David, and Peter, and the rest of these saints, but can you repent with them? Ambrose reproves an Emperor, (who had sinned with David, and was pleading his right to the Lord's supper from this circumstance,) by crying out, " thou hast followed David transgressing, follow David repenting, and then think of the table of the Lord."

The second Remedy is, seriously to consider, that these saints did not make a trade of sinning.

ROMANS vi. 2.
God forbid.

They fell once or twice, (and rose by repentance,) that they might live the closer to Christ forever. They fell through surprisals, accidentally, occasionally, and with much reluctance ; but it may be thou sinnest as a common trade, or sin is by custom become a second nature to thee, which thou canst not, which thou wilt not lay aside, though thou knowest that if thou dost not lay it aside, God will lay thy soul aside forever ; though thou knowest, that if sin and thy soul do not part, Christ and thy soul can never meet. If thou wilt make a trade of sin, and cry out, did not David, and Peter, and other great men do so, knowest thou not that this is a bad mark against thee ? Their hearts turned aside to folly one day, but thy heart every day ; when they fall, they rise through faith and repentance in a crucified Christ; but thou fallest, and hast no strength, no faith, no repentance, nor a crucified Christ to look to.

The third Remedy is, humbly to consider, that though God will not cast off his people forever, yet he will visit their iniquities with severe chastisement.

Psalm lxxxix. 32, 33.
Their iniquity with stripes.

God's corrections are our instructions, his lashes our lessons, his scourges our school-masters, and his chastisements our advertisements. Luther saith, " afflictions are the Christian man's divinity." David sins, and God breaks his bones for his sins. Psal. lxi. 8. The Jews have a proverb, that there is no punishment comes upon Israel in which there is not one ounce of the golden calf : meaning that that was so great a sin, as that in every plague God remembered it, and that it had an influence in every trouble that befel them. Josephus reports, that not long after the Jews had crucified Christ on the cross, so many of them were condemned to be crucified that there were not places enough for crosses, nor crosses enough for the bodies. When Satan shall inform thee of other men's sins, to draw thee to sin, do thou then think of these afflictions and sufferings that they endured on account of their sins, then lay thy hand upon thy heart, and say, oh ! my soul, art thou able to bear these sorrows?

The fourth Remedy is carefully to consider, that the recording of the sins of good men is to accomplish some great end.

JOB xxxiii. 17.

*To draw man from his purpose, and to hide pride
from him.*

The Lord may be said to have designed the
magnifying of his grace and mercy in them that fell;
the preserving the souls of his children from sinking
in despair under the burden of their sins, who fall
through weakness and infirmity : and that their falls
may be as land-marks, to warn others that stand to
take heed lest they fall. It never could be supposed,
for a moment, that God would have recorded the sins
of his people in so pointed and faithful a manner,
that those who should read the account might be encouraged to sin thereby, but rather to evince the purity of the Divine perfections, the honor of the holy
law, the eternal hatred of sin, and the depth of the
riches, both of the wisdom and knowledge of God in
pardoning the soul, yet scourging it for sin, and in
exciting the minds of those that stand to keep the
closer to the skirts of Christ.

The fifth Remedy is, thankfully to consider, that
the excellence and power of God's grace and truth
are the more illustrated, and the evil of sin exposed.

2 CORINTHIANS xii. 9.

I glory in infirmities.

There is an evident excellency in the grace of
God, in its reigning authority and glory over sin and

emptation, through faith in Jesus Christ, hereby making men able to stand out against this mighty adversary; and that notwithstanding all the plots, devices, and stratagems of Satan, grace and truth makes them victorious here, and crowns them with glory hereafter. The greater and subtler the enemy, the more divine wisdom, and power, and goodness shine in preserving his children from a compliance with the snares of the devil. When Paul considered this subject, he revoked his sad conjectures, and took courage to glory in his infirmities, his own weaknesses and distresses, and in Satan's buffetings, that the power of Christ might rest upon him. Thus, though there should not be a just man upon the earth that doeth good and sinneth not, yet there cannot arise the encouragement to any person to live in sin from hence, if we reflect upon the repentance of the saints, or the conduct of God to them under those sins, &c.

The sixth Remedy is seriously to consider, that the society of such men is dangerous.

JUDE 16.
Walking after their own lusts.

Against this fifth device of Satan to draw the soul to sin, from the sins and fallings of good men, be it remembered, that the company of such men, who take encouragement to sin from the sins of the righteous, is ever to be considered as infectious and ruinous to souls. The scriptures speak loudly and most solemnly on this point, in the different names, notions, and characters that the Holy Ghost hath given to such men: take, for instance, this short epistle of Jude, and profit by the relation of them. Ah! my friends, how many have lost their names, their estates, their strength, their God, their heaven, and their souls forever by the society of wicked men! As the seaman shuns the sands, and rocks, and shoals, and as ye would shun the house where the plague dreadfully reigns, so flee from that man or woman that can take liberty to sin from the failings of pious men.

CHAP. VI.

THE SIXTH DEVICE OF SATAN TO DRAW THE SOUL
TO SIN, IS BY PERSUADING THE SOUL, THAT THE
WORK OF REPENTANCE IS AN EASY WORK.

PSALM vi. 2.

Have mercy upon me, O Lord, &c.

WHY, suppose you do sin, saith Satan, its no
such difficult thing to return and confess, and be
sorrowful and ask forgiveness, saying, " have mercy upon me, O Lord!" If you do but this, there
can be no doubt but that God will hear you, quit
the score, pardon your sins, and save your souls ;
upon this repentance you have nothing to fear ; for
the goodness of God is great, and sinners of all
casts and characters have cried for mercy, and
found a ready pardon : and therefore the soul doth
not need to be troubled, nor make so much of sinning, as repentance is so easy a work. By this
artful device Satan draws many souls to sin : and
may be said to make millions slaves to lust : or
frighten them to despair that there is no repentance
for them ; for sometimes, and to some characters, he
represents repentance as a light affair, and anon
he cries it up so high and difficult that few can at-
tain it.

The precious Remedies against this device of Satan are these:

First, Seriously to consider that repentance is a great and difficult work.

JEREMIAH xiii. 23.

Can the Ethiopian change his skin, or the leopard his spots?

There is no power, below that power that raised Jesus Christ from the dead, that can break the heart of a sinner, and turn a sinner by repentance, to God. O man! thou art as well able to melt adamant, as to melt thine own heart: to turn a flint into flesh, as to turn thine own heart to the Lord; to raise the dead, and to make a new world, as to repent. Repentance is a flower that grows not in Nature's garden. Men are not born with repentance in their hearts, as they are with tongues in their mouths. Repentance is a gift that cometh down from above; and there is no man able (by his own power) to repent at pleasure. Fallen man hath lost the command of himself; and therefore he that cannot command himself, cannot repent of himself. As many are undone by buying a counterfeit jewel, so many are in hell by mistaking their repentance.

The second Remedy is, attentively to consider the nature of true repentance.

5*

JEREMIAH xxxi. 18, 19.

Turn thou me and I shall be turned.

Repentance is sometimes taken in a more strict and narrow sense for godly sorrow; sometimes it is taken in a large sense for a change in the person, and in his life. True repentance hath three things, viz. the act—subject—terms.

1. The act of repentance is a turning, a changing, or converting from one thing to another, as from sin to God.

2. The subject changed and converted, is the whole man; 'tis both the sinner's heart and life: first his heart, then his life: his person first, then his practice and conversation.

3. The terms of this change and turning, from which and to which both heart and life must be converted from all sin to God. The heart must be changed from the state and power of sin, and the life from the practice, and both unto God; the heart to be under his power in a state of grace, and the life under his rule in all new obedience. Luther saith, "Repentance for sin is nothing worth, without repentance from sin."

The third Remedy is, solemnly to consider, that repentance includeth a turning from the sweetest and most darling sin.

HOSEA xvi. 8.

Ephraim shall say, what have I to do any more with idols ?

turn over
see page 3-3

Herod turned from many sins, but turned not from his Herodias, which was his ruin. Judas turned from all visible wickedness, yet he would not cast out that golden devil, covetousness, and therefore he was cast into the hottest place in hell. He that turns not from darling sins, turns not aright from any one sin. Every sin strikes at the honor of God, the being of God, the heart of God, the heart of Christ, the joy of the Spirit, and the peace of a man's own conscience. True repentance therefore strikes at all sin, hates all, and conflicts with all ; right eyes and right hands plucks out and cuts off from the real penitent ; for one Agag spared cost Saul his kingdom, and at last his soul. Thus repentance is a great work, and not only includeth a sorrow for sin, but a loathing of a person's self before God, accompanied with a holy shame, and blushing (of the face) at the throne of grace, a longing of the soul to all good things, and a new obedience in life, through faith in Jesus Christ.

The fourth Remedy is, carefully to consider, that repentance is a continued act and exercise, both in heart and life.

PSALM li. 3.

I acknowledge my transgressions, and my sin is ev-
er before me.

Repentance is a grace of God, and it must have
its daily operation as well as other graces. A true
penitent must go on from faith to faith, from
strength to strength : he can never stand still nor
turn back. Repentance is a continued act of turning, a repentance never to be repented of, a turning never to turn again to folly. True penitents
have ever something within them, as well as those
things that are without them, to turn them ; they
are still sensible of sin, and still conflicting with sin ;
still sorrowing, still loathing, and still humbling
themselves before God for their sins : and daily find
that repentance is no transient act, but a continual
act of the soul : therefore tell me, O tempted soul,
whether it be an easy thing, as Satan would make
thee believe, to be every day turning more and more
from sin, and turning nearer and nearer to God, as
thy chiefest good and only happiness. As one act
of faith and love cannot content a believer, so neither can one act of repentance.

The fifth Remedy is, seriously to consider, that
if the work of repentance is so easy as Satan would
represent, then certainly the soul would not cry out
with such terror and horror of conscience for not
repenting.

LUKE xvi. 24, 30.

I am tormented in this flame.—Nay, but if one went unto them from the dead, they would repent.

If repentance be a thing so easy, why should so many lie roaring under the terrors of their conscience for not repenting? Surely so many millions would not perish forever if it were an easy thing to repent. Ah! do not poor souls, under the horrors of their conscience, cry out and say, that were the world a lump of gold, and in their hands to dispose of, they would give it all for the least drop of true repentance? If repentance be so easy, why then do (wicked) men's hearts rise so furiously against the preaching of the doctrine of repentance in the strongest and choicest arguments that the scriptures doth afford? Tell me, O soul! when a poor sinner, whose conscience is awakened, shall judge the exchange of all the world for the least tear of true repentance to be the happiest and noblest exchange ever made, if repentance can be an easy work?

The sixth Remedy is, duly to consider, that to repent of sin is as great a work of grace as not to sin.

2 CORINTHIANS vii. 11.

For behold this self-same thing, &c.

By our sinful fall the powers of the soul are weakened, the strength of grace is decayed, our evidences

for heaven blotted, fears and doubts are raised in the
soul, and corruptions in the heart are advantaged
and confirmed : now for the soul, notwithstanding all
this, to repent of his falls, must shew, that it is a
great work of grace to repent of sin. Christ is the
soul's physician, and repentance is the emetic that
causeth the conscience to throw off its load of sin ;
and Jesus' blood is the healing balm. The same
means that tend to preserve the soul from sin, the
same means work in the soul to rise by repentance
when fallen into sin. *Psal.* xxvi. 3, 4. *Hos.* vi. 1, 2.
Remember, that there is much of the power of God,
love of God, faith in God, fear of God, care to
please God, and zeal for the glory of God, requi-
site to work a man to repent of his sins, as there
is to keep him from sin ; therefore it is as great a
work of the Lord in us to repent truly of sin, as not to
sin ; consequently it is not an easy thing to repent.

CHAP. VII.

THE SEVENTH DEVICE OF SATAN TO DRAW THE SOUL
TO SIN, IS TO MAKE THE SOUL BOLD TO VENTURE
UPON THE OCCASIONS OF SIN.

JOSHUA vii. 21.
*When I saw among the spoils a goodly Babylonish
garment, &c. and a wedge of gold, I coveted.*

YEA, saith Satan, you may walk by the harlot's
door, though you won't go into her bed, there can
be no danger in coming by the house ; you may look
upon Jezebel's beauty, though you do no come near
to her chamber ; you may sit and play upon the lap,
and freely chat with Delilah, though you do not commit wickedness with her ; and with Achan handle
the golden wedge, though you do not steal it. Surely saith Satan, a man may sit, converse, and trade
with other men, although they should not be so religious as he is, and yet receive no harm; for it is not
our being in company, but our heart that can make
us sinners ; therefore we may venture to go by the
way side, and sit and enjoy the lively company of
such men as differ from us, without any danger at
all to our persons and characters.

The precious Remedies against this device of Satan are these :

First. Seriously to consider, that the scriptures expressly forbid us to come near to the occasion of sin.

PROVERBS v. 8.

Remove thy way from her, and come not nigh the door of her house.

The word of God expressly commands us to avoid the occasion of sin, and abstain from the very appearance of evil, and do nothing wherin sin appears, or which hath a shadow of it ; whatsoever is unsound and unsavory shun, as you would a serpent in your way. Theodosius tore the Arian's arguments presented to him in writing, because he found them repugnant to the scriptures ; and Augustine retracted all his ironies, because they had the appearance of lying. It was good counsel that Livia gave her husband Augustus : " It behooveth thee not only to do no wrong, but not to seem to do so." Bernard saith, whatever is of an ill shew, or of ill report, that we may neither wound conscience nor credit, we must shun, and be shy with the very shadow, if we value our credit abroad, or our comfort at home. Jude 23.

The second Remedy is, solemnly to consider, that there can be no conquest over sin without the soul turns from the occasion of sin.

PSALM i. 1.

Blessed is the man that walketh not in the council of the ungodly.

As long as the human heart carries its own fuel for every temptation, we cannot be secure : for he that taketh gunpowder with him had need keep at a distance from the sparks. To rush upon the occasions of sin, is both to tempt ourselves and to tempt Satan to tempt our souls. It is very rare that any soul plays with the occasions of sin, but that soul is insnared by sin; yea, it is morally impossible for that man to get the conquest of sin, that daily sports and plays with the occasions of sin. He that adventures upon the occasions of sin, is as one that would attempt to quench the fire with oil, which is as fuel to inflame and increase its rage. Ah! souls, often remember how frequently you have been overcome by sin when you have boldly ventured upon the occasion. Look back, and view the days of your vanity, wherein you have been as easily conquered as tempted; vanquished as assaulted. If you would be victorious over sin, oh! flee from the occasion of sin.

6

The third Remedy is, attentively to consider, that the children of God have turned away from the occasions of sin, as from sin itself.

JOB xxxi. 1.

I have made a covenant with mine eyes, &c.

I set a watch at the entrance of my senses, that my soul might not by them be infected and endangered. The eye is the window of the soul, if that should always be open, the soul must smart for it. The Heathens would not look upon beauty, lest they should be insnared. Democritus plucked out his own eyes to avoid the danger of uncleanness. The Nazarite might not only not drink wine, but he must not taste a grape, or the lush of a grape. The leaper was to shave his hair and to pare his nails, to take away all occasion of danger. Satan counts a fit occasion half a conquest, for he knows that corrupt nature hath a seed-plot of all sin, which being once drawn forth and watered by sinful occasions, is soon set to work, to the producing of death and destruction.

The fourth Remedy is, diligently to consider that to depart from the occasion of sin is a strong evidence of the grace of God in us.

PSALM xix. 12,13.

Keep back thy servant from presumptive sins; then
shall I be upright.

That the avoiding the occasions of sin is an unde-
niable evidence of grace, and that which exalts a man
above most other men in the world. He is a man of
grace indeed, who, when in temptation, and when
sinful occasions present themselves before the soul,
can nobly withdraw himself from the snare: this
speaks out both the truth and the strength of his
grace, when with Lot a man can be chaste in Sodom;
with Job can walk uprightly in the land of Uz; with
Timothy can live temperately in Asia, among the
luxurious Ephesians; and, with Daniel and his companions, lead an holy life amongst the profane and
superstitious Babylonians. Many a man is big and
full of sinful corruption, but shews it not, for want
of an opportunity to favor his lust: but that man
must surely be good, who, when the most favorable
occasions to sin are given him, still avoids the evil.
Therefore, as you would cherish a precious evidence
of grace in your own souls, shun all occasion to sin.

The fifth Remedy is, seriously to consider, that by
closer communion with God we shall prevail both
against sin and the occasions of sin.

1 John i. 7.

If we walk in the light, we have fellowship one with another.

Our strength to stand and withstand all Satan's fiery darts is from our nearness to God : a soul high in communion with God may be tempted, but will not easily be conquered ; for this communion is the result of our union, and a reciprocal exchange between Christ and a gracious soul. Communion is Jacob's ladder, where you have Christ coming down into the soul, and the soul sweetly ascending up to Christ, by the divine influences. Adam loseth his communion with God, and is overcome through the snare of the devil. Sampson, David, Job, and Peter, whilst they kept up communion with God, no enemy could stand before them ; for Job conquered even upon the dunghill. Thus communion with God furnisheth the soul with the greatest and the choicest arguments to turn away from the bold ventures and occasions of sin.

The sixth Remedy is, carefully to consider, that whenever sin, or the occasions of sin, do attempt to draw us to a compliance, we should call for fresh strength from Christ.

John xv. 5.

For without me ye can do nothing.

Certainly for the soul not to be taken in by the occasions of sin, but manfully to stand out and conquer, supposeth the soul daily to be receiving new supplies from Jesus Christ. Oh! saith the soul, I see a new snare laid to catch my soul, and the grace, resolution, and ability I had for the former one will not do for this ; give me new strength, new power, new influence, and new measures of grace, that I may escape this sad snare also. Ah! souls, consider that your strength to stand and overcome the occasions of sin, must not be expected from graces received, but from the fresh and renewed influences of heaven : you must lean more upon Christ than upon spiritual tastes and discoveries, or Satan will lead you captive by this device, in emboldening you to venture upon the occasions of sin.

6*

CHAP. VIII.

THE EIGHTH DEVICE OF SATAN TO DRAW THE SOUL TO SIN, IS BY REPRESENTING THE PROSPERITY AND MERCIES THAT ATTEND THE WICKED.

JEREMIAH xliv. 16, 17, 18.

For then had we plenty, and were well, and saw no evil.

OH ! soul, saith Satan, dost thou not see the many mercies that such and such enjoy, who walk in those ways that thy soul startles to think of; and how many crosses they are delivered from, even such as make other men spend their days in sighing, weeping, groaning, and mourning ? And therefore, saith Satan, if thou wouldst be freed from the dark night of adversity, and walk in the sunshine of prosperity, thou must come forth and walk cheerfully in the ways of such men as never knew adversity : thus should all things go well with you in this world, and your souls be preserved from those distressing fears and afflictions that bring down the strength and sink the spirits of religious men.

The precious Remedies against this device of Satan are these :

First. Carefully to consider, that no man can know either the love or the hatred of God by all outward things.

ECCLESIASTES ix. 1, 2.
All things come alike to all.

Seriously consider that no man knows how the heart of God stands by his hands : his hand of mercy may be towards a man, when his heart is against him ; as you see in Saul : and the hand of God may be set against a man when his heart is dearly set upon him ; as you see in Job and Ephraim ; the hand of God were sorely set against them, and yet the heart and bowels of God were strongly working towards them. No man then, can know either the love or the hatred of the Lord by outward mercy or misery ; for all things come alike to all, to the righteous and to the unrighteous, to the good and to the bad, and to the clean and to the unclean. The sun of prosperity shines as well upon the brambles of the wilderness, as upon the fruit-trees in the orchard ; the snow and hail of adversity lights upon the best garden, as well as upon a stinking dunghill. Saul and Jonathan were different characters in life, yet in their deaths were not divided. Health, wealth, honor, crosses, losses and sicknesses, are cast upon good and bad men promiscuously ; and in general the worst of men have the most of this world, and the best men the least.

The second Remedy, is seriously to consider, that wicked men are the most needy men in the world.

ESTHER v. 12, 13.
Yet all this availeth me nothing.

It is true the wicked have honors, riches, pleasures, and friends, and are mighty in power; their seed is established in the earth, and their hearts are lifted up and grown big through the thoughts of their abundance, and their eyes stand out with fatness; neither are they in trouble like other men : yet all this is nothing to what they want—they want an interest in God, Christ, the Spirit, the promises, the covenant of grace, and the everlasting glory; they want acceptance and reconciliation with God ; they want righteousness, justification, sanctification, and adoption, through Jesus Christ our Lord ; they want pardon of sin, power, freedom, and dominion over all sin.   A crown of gold cannot cure the head-ache, nor a velvet slipper ease the gout ; so neither can all the glory of this world still the conscience. The heart may be compared to a triangle, which the whole round circle of the world cannot fill, but the corners would complain, and cry out for something else. But Oh! the wants of such men that are without God.

The third Remedy is, solemnly to consider, that outward things are not as they seem and are esteemed by vain men.

PSALM lxxiii. 3.

I was envious at the foolish when I saw the prosperity of the wicked, &c. &c.

They have, indeed, a glorious outside ; but when you view their insides, you will soon find that they fill the head full of cares and the heart full of fears. What if the fire should consume one part of my estate, and the sea should swallow up another part? What if my servants should be unfaithful abroad, and my children deceitful at home? It was a good saying of Augustine, "Many are miserable by loving hurtful things, but they are more miserable by having them." It was a noble speech of an Emperor, "You gaze on my purple robe and golden crown, but did you know what cares are under it, you would not stoop to take it up from the ground tho' you might have it for that." Ah! the secret frettings, vexings, and gnawings that do daily, yea, and hourly attend those men's souls whose hands and hearts are full of this world's goods ; therefore, it is not what a man enjoys, but the principle from whence it comes, that can make men happy. If God gives them in his wrath, and does not sanctify them in his love, they will be swift witnesses against a man for the abuse of these good things.

The fourth Remedy is, attentively to consider the end and the design of God in heaping up mercy without misery upon the head of the wicked.

EXODUS ix. 16.
For this cause have I raised thee up. &c.

God's setting them up is but in order to his casting them down ; his raising them high is but in order to his bringing them low, that he may let fly at them his arrows, and pursue them safely, and overtake them with his sore judgments, that his name may be great in Israel, when he has brought down the pride, power, pomp, and glory of the wicked. The Emperor Valens fell from his throne, to be a footstool to Sapor, King of Persia; Dyonisius fell from his kingly glory, to be a schoolmaster; and how did the Lord bring down the rage and glory of Pharoah, king of Egypt! There is not a wicked man or woman in the world that is lifted up, with Lucifer, as high as heaven, but shall, with him, be brought down as low as hell. O Lord, make me rather gracious, than great; inwardly holy, rather than outwardly happy ; little in this world, that I may be great in another ; low here, that I may be high forever hereafter : yea, let me be now clothed

with rags, and at last decked with thy robes, rather
than set up for a time, that thou mayest bring me
low forever. Psal. xcii. 7.

The fifth Remedy is, humbly to consider, that
God doth often most singularly plague and punish
those whom we are ready to think he loveth most.

PSALM cvi. 15.

He gave them their request, but sent leanness into
their souls.

The Lord doth plague and punish with spiritual
judgments (which are the greatest and sorest of all
calamities) them whom he seems to punish the least
with temporals. There are no men on earth so internally plagued as those that meet with the least external plague. Who can describe the blindness of
mind, the hardness of heart, the searedness of conscience, that those men are given up to, who, in the
eye of the world, are reputed the most happy, because they are not afflicted, and in trouble, as other
men? My friends, nothing can better or move that
man who is given up to spiritual judgments : let life
or death, heaven or hell, be set before him, it stirs
him not: he is made up in his sins, and God is fully
set to do justice upon his soul. This man's treasures and preservations are but his fuel and reserva-
tion unto greater condemnation. It is better to have
a sore, than a seared conscience; it is better to have

no heart, than a hard heart ; yea, it is better to have no mind than to have a blind mind. Oh ! 'tis a heavy plague to have a fat body and a lean soul ; a house full of gold, and a heart full of sin.

The sixth Remedy is, solemly to consider, that there is no greater misery in this life, than for a man to go unpunished.

HEBREWS xii. 8.

If ye be without chastisement, then are ye bastards, and not sons.

There is no greater misery in this life, than not to be in misery ; no greater affliction, than not to be afflicted. Woe, woe to the soul that God will not spend a rod upon. This is the saddest stroke of any when God refuses to strike at all. When the physician gives over the patient, you say there is no hope, the man is dead ; so when God gives over a soul to sin without afflictions or control, you may say that that man is a bastard, and no son of God ; for he is as dead to God and happiness, as the man whose knell is rung. Freedom from the rod is the mother of carnal security. Nothing, saith one, seems more unhappy to me, than he to whom no adversity hath happened. Outward mercies and prosperity are oftentimes stumbling blocks, at which millions have stumbled, and fallen eternally. " I will lay a stumbling block." Ezek. iii. 20. Vatablus, in his notes, saith thus, "I will prosper him in all things, and not by afflictions restrain him from sin." The heart of man is like a top, that will not go unless it be whipped, and the more you whip it the better it goes. Bees are killed with honey, but quickened with vinegar; so does the honey of prosperity kill the soul, and the vinegar of correction quicken our spirits.

7

CHAP. IX.

THE NINTH DEVICE OF SATAN TO DRAW THE SOUL TO SIN, IS BY REPRESENTING TO IT THE CROSSES, LOSSES, AND DAILY REPROACHES AND EVILS THAT ATTEND THOSE WHO WALK IN THE WAYS OF HOLINESS.

HEBREWS x. 33.

A gazing-stock both by reproaches and afflictions.

SAITH Satan, do you not see that there are none in all the world that are so hard set, vexed and afflicted and tossed about, as those that walk more circumspectly and holily than their neighbors? They are a by-word at home, and a reproach abroad; their miseries come in upon them like Job's messengers, one upon the neck of another, and there is no end of their sorrows and troubles; therefore saith Satan you had better walk in the ways of the worldly good man, where there are less crosses, losses, and afflictions, than to be so very religious and circumspect; for who but a madman would spend all his days in sorrow, vexation and sore travail and contempt, when he might prevent all this weight of affliction by walking in the way of his forefathers and his neighbors, whom he seeth to live in peace, who are far from trouble?

The precious Remedies against this device of Satan are these:

First. Seriously to consider, that all the afflictions that attend the righteous shall tend to their instruction and profit.

ISAIAH i. 25.

I will turn my hand upon thee, and purely purge away thy dross.

Crosses, losses, and afflictions are the Christian's glass, wherein the soul hath the clearest sight of the ugly face of sin; and views it not only as sin, but as the greatest evil in the world, yea, worse than hell itself. By these afflictions God mortifies and purgeth away the sins of his people; they serve as his furnace, to cleanse and refine from their dross and tin; it is a potion to carry away all bad humors, better than all the *benedicta medicamentum* of physicians. Aloes kill worms; colds and frosts destroy vermin; so do afflictions the corruptions of the heart: they have also a preserving and preventing good to all his saints. Afflictions are sweet preservatives to keep the saints from sin; as the burnt child dreads the fire, so the child of God dreads sinning more than hell. Salt preserves from putrefaction; and salt marshes keep the sheep from the rot: so doth affliction keep the saints from sin.

The second Remedy is, carefully to consider, that afflictions are but inlets to the soul of the more abundant sweets, and full enjoyment of God and divine truth in this world.

Hosea ii. 14.

I will bring her into the wilderness, and speak comfortably unto her.

The flowers smell sweetest after a shower: vines bear the better for bleeding; the walnut-tree is most fruitful when most beaten: so the saints spring and thrive most internally, when they are most externally afflicted. When was it that God appeared in his glory to Jacob, and favored his soul with more than common inlets of joy and transport, but in the days of his trouble, when the stone was his pillow, the ground his bed, and the heavens his canopy? When did Stephen see the heavens open, and Christ standing at the right hand of God, but when the stones were about his head and ears, and there was but a short step betwixt him and eternity? The plant in Nazianzen grows by cutting, lives by dying, and by cutting flourishes the more: so saints by their losses, gain more experience of the power of God to support them, the wisdom of God to direct them, and the grace of God to refresh them.

The third Remedy is, solemnly to consider, that the afflictions of the saints only reach the body.

LUKE xii. 4.

Be not afraid of them that kill the body, &c.

The afflictions that befal the people of God reach their worst part, but touch not nor hurt their noble part; all the arrows stick fast in the target, they reach not the conscience.   And who shall harm you if ye be followers of that which is good?   They may afflict you, but shall never harm you.   It was a good saying of an heathen, who when a tyrant commanded him to be put into a mortar, and beaten to pieces with an iron pestle, cried out, " You do but beat the vessel, the case, the husk of Anaxarchus : you beat not me."   The body is but the case, the vessel or the husk ; the soul is the man which they cannot reach.   Socrates said to his enemies, you may kill me, but you cannot harm me ; so say the children of God to their afflictions, crosses, losses, and temptations, you may kill us, but you cannot harm us ; you may take away life, but cannot take away our God, our Christ, or our crown.

The fourth Remedy is, attentively to consider, that the afflictions of the righteous are short and momentary.

PSALM xxx. 5.

Weeping may endure for a night, but joy cometh in the morning.

Those light afflictions, which are but for a mo-

7*

ment, will end in everlasting joy. It is but a very short space between grace and glory : between our title to the crown, and our wearing the crown ; between our right to the heavenly inheritance and our possession of the heavenly inheritance. What is our life, but a shadow, a bubble, a flower, a post, a span, and as a dream in the night. Luther was at a loss to find diminutives to express its shortness. The prophet (Isa. xxvi. 20) saith it is but a little moment. Athanasius, in his misery, said to his friends, when they wept over him, " It is but a little cloud, and will quickly be gone." 'Twill be but as a day before God will give his afflicted ones beauty for ashes; the oil of gladness for the spirit of heaviness; before he will turn all their sighing into singing, all our lamentations to consolations, our sackcloth into silks, ashes into ointments, and our fasts into everlasting feasts : these all work for us a far more exceeding and eternal weight of glory.

The fifth Remedy is, joyfully to consider, that all afflictions to the saints proceed from God's love to them.

REVELATIONS iii. 19.
As many as I love I rebuke.

To the saints God saith, think not that I hate you, because I thus chide you. He that escapes reprehension, may suspect his adoption. God had one

Son without corruption, but no son without correction. A gracious soul may look through the darkest cloud and see his God smiling on him : we must therefore look through the anger of his corrections to the sweetness of his countenance ; and as by a rainbow we see the beautiful image of the sun's light in the midst of a dark and watery cloud, so the love of God to the soul is known by the cloud of affliction. A soul, at first conversion, is but a rough cast ; but God by afflictions, doth square, and fit, and polish it for that glorious building, where it shall appear as a lively stone, growing up to an holy temple for the Lord. Therefore afflictions spring from God's love to the soul, and can be no bar to holiness, nor any motive to draw the soul to the works and ways of the wicked.

The sixth Remedy is, studiously to consider that we should not measure the afflictions of the saints by the smart, but by the end of them.

Genesis xv. 13, 14.
They shall come out with great substance.

Israel was in bondage and affliction four hundred years in Egypt ; but they were dismissed with gold and ear-rings ! Israel was seventy years in Babylon, covered with sorrows, but came out with gifts, jewels, and every needful thing ! Look more at the latter end of a christian, than at the beginning of his afflictions. Look not at the beginning of Joseph's sorrows, and his dreams, but behold him, after he had passed through the sea, set upon the throne, and made ruler over all the land of Egypt. Consider the patience of Job, and what was the end of the Lord to him. Look not upon David when his life was hunted like a partridge upon the mountain, but behold him established upon the throne of Israel. Look not at Lazarus' sores, but at his sweet repose in Abraham's bosom. Afflictions that attend the righteous ways of God, are but as a dirty lane to a royal palace, and as a dark entry to our father's house; we will therefore walk in wisdom's ways.

CHAP. X.

THE TENTH DEVICE OF SATAN TO DRAW THE SOUL
TO SIN, IS BY DEFILING THE SOULS AND JUDG-
MENTS OF MEN WITH DANGEROUS ERRORS.

1 JOHN iv. 6.
The spirit of error.

HOW numerous, harmonious, courageous, and active are Satan's faithful subjects to sow the seeds of
error, aided by their great lord and master, in his
unwearied attempts to destroy the souls of men!
Satan, by polluting and defiling the souls and judgments of men with dangerous errors, doth ruin thousands, who are ignorant of his devices. How active
is Satan in spreading all manner of error against
the doctrine of the Trinity, the divinity of Jesus
Christ, the necessity of divine teaching, the resurrection of the dead, the glory of heaven, and the torments of hell; and, with a plausible pretence to piety, through affected courtesy, and fawning flattery
and smoothness, entice multitudes to spiritual whore-
dom; and for carnal advantage reject, corrupt, and
misapply the oracles of God; and with shifts, eva-
sions, and self-inconsistencies, spoil God's vineyard,

unsettle weak and young professors, ruin the souls
of men, and promote the kingdom of darkness?

The precious Remedies against Satan's devices to
defile the soul with error are these:

First. To consider, that an erroneous mind is as
offensive to God as a vicious life.

JUDE 11.

*Woe unto them! for they ran greedily after the er-
ror of Balaam.*

He that had the leprosy in his head was to be pro-
nounced utterly unclean. Gross errors make the
heart foolish, and render the life loose and the soul
light in the eyes of God. Error spreads and frets
like a gangrene, and renders the soul a leper in the
sight of God. It was God's heavy and dreadful
plague upon the Gentiles, to be given up to a mind
void of judgment; a mind rejected, disallowed, and
abhorred of God; an injudicious mind, and a mind
that none have any cause to glory in, but rather to
be ashamed of. A blind eye is worse than a lame
foot. The breath of the erroneous is infectious;
and, like the dogs of Cango, they bite, though they
will not bark. To persist in error, in the open face
of truth, is diabolical. They must needs err who
know not the ways of God; yet can they not wan-
der so wide as to miss of hell.

The second Remedy is, to receive the truth affectionately, that we may be saved.

2 THESSALONIANS ii. 10, 11, 12.
Because they received not the love of the truth, &c.

Let the truth of God dwell in us plenteously. When men stand out against the truth, and bar the door of their souls against the conviction of truth, God in justice gives them up to be deluded and deceived by error, to their eternal ruin. Ah! souls, if you have love to yourselves, do not tempt God to give you up to believe a lie, that you may be damned. There are no men on earth so fenced against error, as those are who receive the truth in love. It is not our receiving the truth into our heads, but the receiving it into our hearts, that can give us the happiness to enjoy clear and sound judgments, while others go on deluded, and deceive both themselves and others with the errors of the wicked; until all fall into the dyke together. Oh! my friends, as you would not have your judgments polluted and defiled with errors concerning your temporal, why should you suffer yourselves to be led into the snares of the devil concerning your spiritual estate?

The third Remedy is, seriously to consider, that error is without profit or reward.

1 CORINTHIANS iii. .11, 12, 13, 14, 15.
The fire shall try it, &c.

All the pains and labor that men take to defend
and maintain their errors, to spread abroad and infect the world therewith, shall bring neither profit
nor comfort to them in that day when the fire shall
try every man's work, of what sort it is: then all
those that rise early and go to bed late, that spend
their time, their strength, their spirits, and their all
to support, advance, and spread abroad God dishonoring and soul-ruining opinions, shall find that they
now must lose all the pains, cost, and charges which
they have been put to for the propagation of their
pernicious errors. Ah! sirs, is it nothing to you
to lay out your money for that which is not bread,
and your strength for that which satisfieth not, nor
can profit you in that day when you must give up
your accounts, and your works be tried with fire?
Cæsar loved his books more than his royal robes:
when he was forced to swim through some water,
he carried his books above it, and lost his robes.
Ah! what are Cæsar's books to God's book?

The fourth Remedy is, solemnly to hate and reject all opinions that are contrary to real godliness.

Psalm cxix. 104.

Through thy precepts I get understanding, therefore
I hate every false way.

To abominate, and turn from all those doctrines
and opinions that are contrary to godliness, and that
open a door to profaneness ; and all such doctrines
and opinions that require men to hold forth a stiffness
above what the scriptures have recommended ; and
all such doctrines and opinions that do advance and
lift up corrupt nature to do those things (of themselves) which require supernatural power and grace;
all such opinions and doctrines which establish a
righteousness in man, contrary to the righteousness
of God ; also all those doctrines and opinions which
do set up Christ and his righteousness, and cry down
all duties and holiness in believers ; and finally, all
those doctrines and opinions that are designed to set
the soul against the purity and spirituality of the holy law of God. Thus let our souls arise with an
holy hatred against every thing that sets itself against
God and his holy word.

The fifth Remedy is, carefully to cherish a lowly
and teachable disposition before the word of God.

Psalm cxix. 129, 130, 131.

The entrance of thy word giveth light, it giveth un-
derstanding to the simple.

A teachable disposition to the divine word will
keep the soul free from many devices which Satan

casts in the way of truth. As low trees and shrubs are free from many violent gusts and blasting winds, which shake and rend the taller trees, so humble, teachable souls are freed from those gusts and blasts of errors, that rend and tear proud, lofty, and conceited souls. The God of light and truth delights to dwell with the lowly and teachable: and the more light and truth dwells in the soul, at the greater distance must darkness and error be kept: and the God of grace pours grace into the humble soul, as we pour water into empty vessels; and the more grace is poured into the soul, the less error shall be able to overpower, or to infect the principles within the soul. The highest tide quickly ebbs, and the highest sun is presently declining; it is just so with all high and exalting notions in men, who set themselves to pervert the way of life. "Though I cannot dispute for the truth, yet I can die for the truth," said a martyr.

The sixth Remedy is, seriously to consider, that error has produced great evil in this world.

JOHN xvi. 2.

Whosoever killeth you, will think that he doeth God service.

Errors in judgment and conscience have produced infinite evils, not only in men's own souls, but also in human affairs. Error is a fruitful mother, and hath brought forth such monstrous children, as have set whole towns, cities, nations, congregations, families, and individuals all on fire and in confusion, in former days; and it were to be desired that in our time there were not too just reason to complain of monsters in religion, that think they do God service in laying waste the heritage of Jacob. Oh! the graces that error hath weakened, and the sweet joys and comforts that error hath clouded, if not buried! Oh! the hands that error hath shortened, the eyes error hath blinded, the judgments of men that error hath perverted, the hearts that error hath hardened, the consciences that error hath seared, and the souls that error hath sent to hell! Therefore when Satan would defile and pollute your souls and judgments, by dangerous errors, seriously consider the loss that must inevitably attend a compliance.

CHAP. XI.

THE ELEVENTH DEVICE OF SATAN TO DRAW THE
SOUL TO SIN IS BY WORKING MEN UP TO COMPARE
THEMSELVES WITH THOSE THAT ARE WORSE THAN
THEY.

LUKE xviii. 11.

God, I thank thee, that I am not as other men.

Oh! saith Satan, though we must ever acknowledge that there wanteth not sin in the best of men,
and although your sins do greatly exceed the sins of
good men, yet there is no cause for any distress on
that head, when you look around upon the thousands that are greater sinners than yourself. You
are no extortioner, nor unjust, nor an adulterer, nor
even as this publican. You may bless God that you
was not born a Gentile, are not a swearer, a drunkard, a Sabbath breaker, nor an unclean and lustful
man. Why, saith Satan you swear, but petty oaths,
as by your faith and troth, &c. but you know that
neighbor such-a-one swears stoutly by his God.—
You now and then are a little merry : but such and
such are profanely wanton. You may deceive and
over-reach in things that are but toys and trifles ;
but you know those who deceive and over-reach
others in things of the greatest moment, even to

their utter ruin : therefore cheer up, you are not only not worse than your neighbors, but you are better than they.

–––––––––

The precious Remedies against this device of Satan are these :

First. Seriously to consider, that for a person to be frequently comparing himself with those that are worse than he, is a proof of hypocrisy.

MATTHEW vii. 5.

First cast out the beam out of thine own eye, &c.

There needeth no clearer argument to prove a person a hypocrite, than to be quick-sighted abroad, and blind at home; than to use spectacles to behold other men's sins, rather than a looking glass to behold his own. I have read of some artful witches, who, when stirring abroad, would put on their eyes, but when returning home would box them up again : so applies my text. Thou hypocrite, first open thy eyes upon thine own sins, then look abroad if thou canst. How apt are such persons to hold their fingers upon other men's sores, magnifying and aggravating them, when they can lessen and smooth their own to the eye of the world ! Hypocrites pray to God only in time of affliction and danger ; they show much love to God, to religion, when pros-

8*

perity smiles upon them; they are more for outward ceremonies and human traditions, than for
pure spiritual worship: they are open-eyed to
worldly affairs, but blind to divine. Oh! my
friends, be afraid of hypocrisy: oh! buy the truth
and by no means sell it, for your soul's sake.

The second Remedy is, solemnly to consider, that
the sin of hypocrisy is difficultly cured.

Luke xii. 1; 2, 3.
Beware ye of the leaven of the Pharisees.

The difficulty of a cure for hypocrisy lies in the
sin not being easily discovered by men, and that it
does not expose to shame, but is made subservient
to many carnal ends. For what man can dive into
the depth of the human heart, and there discern between the paint of hypocrisy and the life of holiness? And besides this, hypocrisy can turn the very means of salvation into poison, to the persons
who use them; for the frequent exercise of religious
duties, which is the means of sanctifying and saving
others, the same means confirm and harden hypocrites. The effectual means to cure hypocrisy, is a
solemn and steadfast belief of the pure and all-see-
ing eye of God, who sees sin wherever it is, and
will bring it into judgment. An hypocrite may
hide his sins from the eyes of others, and sometimes
from his own conscience, but can never impose upon

God: therefore the steadfast belief of the truth will cause frequent and solemn thoughts of God, and incite you to look up to him as your inspector, and judge.

The third Remedy is, carefully to spend more time in comparing ourselves with the scriptures.

JOHN v. 39.

Search the scriptures, for in them ye think ye have eternal life.

To spend more time in comparing ourselves both internal and external, with the divine rule, we should find a remedy sufficiently powerful against this device of Satan. That man, who by comparing himself with others that are worse than he is, may seem, to himself and to others, to be an angel, yet, by searching the scriptures, and comparing himself with the word that shall judge him at the last, will see himself to be like the devil; for the nearer we draw to the world, the more we stir up the vermin that lurk within the heart. The more steadfast a person looks upon the face of the sun, the less beauty and perfection he sees below. It is said of the basilisk, that if he looks into a glass and beholds himself, he presently dies; so will sin and a sinner in a spiritual sense, when the soul looks into the glass of God's word, and compares himself with its purity. Oh! that you and I may see what monstrous things sin and our hearts are, that we may die unto sin and live unto God, through Jesus Christ.

The fourth Remedy is, attentively to consider, that such comparison betrays us to be strangers to God and to ourselves.

JOB xxii. 21.
Acquaint thyself with him and be at peace.

The man that passeth his time away in comparing himself with others, and strives to quiet his conscience with his neighbor's sins being greater than his, giveth sufficient evidence that he is a stranger to God, to the true knowledge of him in Jesus Christ, to the fear and love of God, to his converting grace, and to his nature, offices, righteousness, and work; a stranger to the way of peace, life, holiness, and salvation through him; to faith in, love to, and communion with him: a stranger to the Holy Ghost in his divine person, in his work of regeneration, sanctification, and comfort; and a stranger to himself, to the evils of his own heart and life, to the deceitfulness and exceeding sinfulness of sin: never pricked to the heart for sin; never was its filthiness discovered, or the hardness removed; never to loath himself in his own eyes, or to renounce his own righteousness, and to cast himself at Jesus' feet for mercy and salvation.

The fifth remedy is, seriously to consider, that without true repentance, and the pardoning love of God to us in particular, we shall still come short of eternal life, although we were better than others.

EZEKIEL xvi. 63.
Never open thy mouth any more because of thy shame, when I am pacified.

The soul should never open his mouth to justify self, nor to condemn others; but like a true penitent, be silent under the rod, which his sins have justly deserved, and God hath inflicted, in wisdom, to draw his soul from vain conceit, and confidence in his moral excellencies and comparisons with other men. Divine mercy and repentance bring down the high and lofty soul to submit to God and to give him glory; yea such a confusion 'for thy sins will cover thee, that thou wilt readily approve the word of truth, and justify God in that description of thy own heart; and thou shalt blush at the remembrance of thy own secret wickedness, when God shall reveal his pardoning love and mercy to thy soul, in the day that he is pacified towards thee. Ah! sirs, then ye shall no more live upon comparisons, nor disparisons, but live to sound aloud that saving love, and sing that bleeding heart.

The sixth Remedy is, solemnly to consider those names and characters which Jesus Christ has given to those who are pure in their own eyes, and live upon comparisons.

MATTHEW xxiii. 1—33.
How can ye escape, &c.

Whomsoever they may be that would find a remedy against this device of Satan, let them but attend to the scripture names and characters given to self-righteous persons, and, in particular, consider the chapter referred to above, and they must certainly obtain strong convictions of the danger of the temptations presented by Satan in the eleventh device to draw the soul to sin. It is not safe to look upon men in the names and notions that they set themselves forth by, nor the flattering titles they assume; our Lord still calls them hypocrites, blind guides, fools, whited sepulchres, serpents, generation of vipers, that cannot escape the damnation of hell. Do not tell me then what this man calls himself, or how you account of him, but inform me what the scriptures say of him, and how they vindicate his character. As Nabal's name was, so was his nature; and as those men's names are in scripture, so are their natures and lives before God.

CHAP. XII.

THE TWELFTH DEVICE OF SATAN TO DRAW THE SOUL TO SIN, IS BY REPSESENTING THE GLORY OF THE WORLD.

LUKE iv. 6.

All this power will I give thee, and the glory of them.

SATAN sheweth the beauty, bravery, and glory of the world, to ensnare and win upon the affections of the soul to sin: see, saith he, all this consequence, riches, glory, and honor will I give unto thee, if thou wilt but love and follow me. It is true, this took not with Christ, because Satan could not find matter in him to work upon; but it is not so with us; he can no sooner cast the golden bait, but we are ready to play with, and nibble at it; he no sooner casts out the golden ball, but we run after it to the loss of God and our souls. The beauty of the world soils a christian more than the strength of it; the flattering sunshine, more than the blustering storm: for in storms we keep our garments close about us. Ah! the time, the thoughts, the spirits, the hearts, the souls, the duties, and the strength that the inordinate love of the world hath eaten up and destroyed. Where one thousand are destroyed by the world's frowns, ten thousand have fallen by its smiles. The inhabitants of Nilus are deaf, by reason of the noise of the waters; so the world rings such charms in men's ears, that they are deaf and blind to the voice and ways of God.

———

The precious Remedies against this device of Satan are these:

First. Attentively to consider the impotence and weakness of the world.

James v. 2, 3.

Riches are corrupted, gold and silver are cankered.

All the riches and glory in the world cannot secure us from the least evil, neither are they able to procure us the least desirable good. The crown of gold cannot cure nor prevent the head ache; the velvet slipper cannot ease, nor cure the gout; and the jewels about the neck cannot take away the pain of the teeth. The frogs and plagues of Egypt entered into the houses of the rich, as well as the poor. Our daily experience doth testify, that all the riches in the world that men enjoy cannot free them from the least diseases; nay, what may seem more strange is, they cannot keep men from falling into the greatest extremes of poverty and distress. Look at the royal picture, Judges i. 6. and mark a conqueror,

who, having taken seventy kings, and subdued them
to his own pleasure, forcing them to gather their
bread under his table, with their fingers and toes cut
off, is himself at last taken and brought to the same
poverty and misery that he had inflicted upon others.
Let us then remember the impotency and weakness
of all the world, could we obtain the whole.

The second Remedy is, seriously to consider the
vanity of the world.

ECCLESIASTES i. 2.
Vanity of vanities, all is vanity.

This our first parents found, and therefore called
their second son Abel ; that is, vanity. Solomon,
who had tried these things again and again, declar-
eth them all vanity. It is a sad thing to see how
many thousands there are that can speak with Solomon, " vanity of vanity, all is vanity;" yet after all
this can follow after the world, as if there were no
other glory or felicity but what was to be found in
those things they call vanity. When Gilimex, king
of the Vandals, was led in triumph by Belisarius,
he cried out, "Vanity of vanity, all is vanity."
Tell me, ye who say that all things under the sun are
vanity, if you really do believe what you say, why
you spend more thoughts and time on the world than
you do on Christ, heaven, and your own immortal
souls? Why do you neglect your duty towards

God, to get back to the world? Why so eager and lively in the pursuit after the world, and so cold and backward to the things of God? And why are your hearts so glad when the world comes in smiling, and so sad and cast down when it frowns upon you?

The third Remedy is, solemnly to consider, that the riches of the world are uncertain and inconstant.

1 TIMOTHY vi. 17.

Nor trust in uncertain riches.

Man himself is but a dream, a generation of fancy, an empty vanity, and but a curious picture of nothing. All things below the skies are transitory, and as hasty as a strong torrent, a shadow, a ship, a bird, an arrow, and as a post that passeth by. No man can promise himself to be rich: one storm at sea, one coal of fire, one false friend, one unadvised word, and one false witness, may make thee a beggar and a prisoner all at once. Where is the glory of Solomon? The sumptuous buildings of Nebuchadnezzar? The nine hundred chariots of Sisera? The power of Alexander? The authority of Augustus, who commanded the whole world to be taxed? The most renowned Frederick lost all, and applied to be made but the sexton of the church he had built! Those who have been most glorious and excellent in things of this life, have come down from all with loss: as Sampson, for strength; Absalom for beauty; Ashithophel, for policy; and Haman for favor. So the Chaldean, Persian, Grecian, Roman; and so the present shakings and convulsions, that have impoverished and laid waste ten thousands. Love not the world.

The fourth Remedy is, carefully to consider, that the riches of the world are dangerous.

DEUTERONOMY xxxii. 15.
Jeshurun waxed fat, and then he forsook God.

That the great things of this world are very hurtful and dangerous to the outward and inward man, through the corruptions of the heart, is too plain to be denied: they often swell the heart with pride, and make a man forget God, and so to despise the rock of his salvation. How do they abate our love to God, to his people, to his ordinances, and steal our spirits from sweet communion above! And what, alas! what deadness, barrenness, and leanness of soul attend the love of the world! Henry the second, on hearing that Mentz, his chief city, was taken, blasphemously cried out, "I shall never love God any more, for suffering a city so dear to me to be taken from me." Henry the fourth asked the duke of Alva, if he had observed the great eclipse of the sun? "No," said the Duke, "I have so much to do on earth, that I have no leisure to look up to heaven." Ah! would to God this were not true of too many professors in these days : for the love of money is the root of all evil, which, while some have coveted after they have erred from the faith, and pierced themselves through with many sorrows.

The fifth Remedy is, seriously to consider, that true happiness is not to be found in any worldly good.

ECCLESIASTES v. 10.

He that loveth silver shall not be satisfied with silver.

God is the Christian's chiefest good. True happiness is too great and too glorious to be found in any thing below that good. The glorious angels and spirits above (those glittering courtiers) have their felicities and blessednesses, and yet have they neither gold, nor silver, nor jewels, no, nor any of the beauty and bravery of the world. Real happiness lies only in our enjoyment of a suitable good, a pure good, a total good, and an eternal good : God only is such a good, and therefore God only can satisfy the soul of man. Certainly happiness lies not in those things that a man may enjoy here in this world : if it was so, then a man might be

great and graceless, with Pharoah ; honorable and
damnable, with Saul ; rich and miserable, with Dives,
&c.   Philosophers used to say, that he was never a
happy man who afterwards became miserable. Gregory the Great used to say, " he is a poor man whose
soul is void of grace, not whose coffers are empty of
money."   In short, had there been the least real
happiness in the world, then should the Lord Jesus
Christ have enjoyed a large portion of it himself
while in the world, and he would have granted to his
people the glory of all.

The sixth Remedy is solemnly to acquaint ourselves with better riches and glory than the world.

1 PETER i. 4.
An inheritance incorruptible and undefiled.

Let but heaven be our object, and the world will
soon be our abject. A better acquaintance with,
and better assurance of more blessed and glorious
things above, will raise up our spirits to trample upon all the beauty and glory of the world. The
saints of old took joyfully the spoiling of their goods,
knowing in themselves that they had in heaven a
better and more durable substance ; this made them
count all the glory and bravery of the world to be
too poor and contemptible for them to set their hearts
upon. Luther being at one time in want, a nobleman, unexpectedly, sent him a large sum of money,

at which he was sorely amazed, and cried, " I fear
that God will give me my reward here, but I protest
I will not be satisfied." The main reason why men
dote upon the world and lose their souls, is because
they are unacquainted with the great rewards of
saints above. Oh! did we but live in communion
with God, taste more of heaven, and enjoy more glorious hopes of shortly going to eternal happiness,
how soon should we have this world under our feet?
When Basil was tempted with money and prefer-
ment, he replied, " Give me money that may last forever, and glory that may eternally flourish."

CHAP. XIII.

AS SATAN HATH HIS DEVICES TO DRAW THE SOUL
TO SIN, SO HE HATH HIS DEVICES TO KEEP THE
SOUL FROM HOLY DUTIES; AND HIS FIRST DEVICE
IS BY REPRESENTING THE DIFFICULTY OF PER-
FORMING THEM.

NUMBERS xiii. 31.
We be not able to go up.

How many are turned against the duties of religion, from the formidable difficulties that Satan
casts in the way of performing them aright? Oh!
saith Satan, it is a hard and difficult thing to worship God: thou canst not pray as thou shouldst;
thou art not able to wait upon him, nor to love
him, nor to walk with him, nor to believe on him,
nor to serve him as a true worshipper of God
should; neither art thou lively, warm, and active
in communion with the saints as thou shouldst be;
their souls are zealously attached to the service of
God from principle; they are assisted and encouraged in their worship, so that the difficulty is removed from them, and it becomes a delight to them
to draw near to God,; but as to thee, it is weari-
ness and dejection; therefore it would be better for
thee to give up and neglect those ways that are

neither acceptable to God, from the manner thou performest them, nor yet a pleasure or profit to thyself, in performing them. Thus, no doubt, Satan keeps back thousands from waiting upon the Lord.

The precious Remedies against this device of Satan are these :

First.   Seriously to consider the necessity, more than the difficulty attending divine service.

JOB xxiii. 10, 11, 12.
I have esteemed the words of his mouth more than my necessary food.

Many are the arguments in scripture to awaken us to a sense of the necessity of waiting upon God in holy ordinances : there is a necessary obligation by creation, by providence, and by redemption ; and our souls should reason, that though the service of God should be difficult, yet it is exceeding necessary for the glory of God to keep his worship up in the world, and for keeping under sin, Satan, the world, and an evil heart; for the strengthening of weak graces, the reviving of languishing comforts, the keeping clear and bright our divine evidences, the scattering of our fears, the raising of our hopes, the gladdening of our hearts, and for the stopping of the mouths of the ungodly, who are ready on all occasions to take advantages to blaspheme the name of God, and to reproach both his people and his service. Oh! let us then never leave thinking upon the necessity of all holy duties, until our souls are lifted up far above all the difficulties that attend true religion.

The second Remedy is, carefully to consider, that the Lord Jesus will make his service both easy and delightful.

PHILLIPIANS ii. 13.
For it is God that worketh in you, both to will and
to do.

Consider the Lord Jesus Christ will make his own services easy to his people, by the sweet discoveries of himself to their souls, while in his service ; yea, you shall meet with God who is goodness itself, sweetness itself, beauty itself, strength itself and glory itself. Will not, cannot this sweeten his service to thy soul, and give thee rest? Isaiah lxiv. 5. The Lord will give that sweet assistance, by his spirit and grace, as shall render his service joyful, and not grevious ; a delight and not a burden; a heaven and not a hell, to believing souls. The confidence in this divine assistance raised up the spirits of Nehemiah far above all the difficulties and discouragements that attended him in the work and service of the Lord. Neh. ii. 19, 20. Ah! souls, while you are in the very service of the Lord, you shall find by rich experience, that the God of heaven will prosper and support you, by encouraging, strengthening, and carrying you through the hardest service with the greatest cheerfulness of soul. Remember that they have no cause to fear who have Jesus Christ the conqueror on their side.

The third Remedy is, solemnly to consider that Jesus Christ endured far greater difficulties for our sakes.

HEBREWS xii. 2. 3.
For consider him, &c.

The Lord Jesus Christ hath passed through a sea of blood, a sea of wrath, a sea of sin, and a sea of sorrow and misery, for our good, internal, external, and eternal. Christ did not plead, this cross is too heavy for me to bear; this wrath is too great for me to lie under; this cup, which hath in it all the ingredients of divine displeasure, is too bitter for me to drink, even the very dregs; no, he pleads not the difficulties, but resolutely, cheerfully, and courageously wades through all. Zanch saith, " It is not fit that the members should be crowned with roses, when the head was crowned with thorns." My brethren, if this consideration

will not raise us up above all the discouragements
that Satan, sin, the world, and our own evil heart
can cast in our way, to the service and worship of
God, I am greatly afraid that nothing else can.
A soul not stirred by this, nor raised and lifted up
by this to be resolute and faithful in the service of
God, notwithstanding all difficulties, must be a soul
left of God.

The fourth Remedy is, attentively to consider,
that the difficulties attending the worship of God
are only to the outward man, and not the inward
man.

2 CORINTHIANS iv. 16.

For which cause we faint not, &c.

To the outward man, (which may be called the
ignoble part of a saint,) the heavenly exercises are
only difficult : but they are not to the most noble
part of the christian, the soul : to the nobler part,
holy duties are a heavenly pleasure and a recreation.
I delight in the law of God after the inward man.
The commands of Christ, even those that tend to
putting out of right eyes, and cutting off
right hands, are joyous and not grievous, to the
inward man. A saint, so far as he is renewed, is
always best when he sees most of God, when he
tastes most of God, when he is highest in the enjoyment of God, and most warm and lively in the

service of God.   Oh ! saith the inward man, that
it might be always thus and thus with me ; then
should my strength be as the strength of stones, and
my flesh as brass ; so should my outward man be
more serviceable to my inward ; and though this
my outward man must decay, still should I say,
Christ's yoke is gracious, pleasant, and a profitable
yoke to my soul.

The fifth Remedy is, seriously to consider, that
there is a great reward belonging to the service of
God.

ECCLESIASTES, viii. 12.
It shall be well with them that fear God, &c.

There is a great and glorious recompence attending those that cleave to the service of the Lord in
the face of all difficulties and discouragements :
therefore, though the work be hard, yet the wages
are great, heaven will make ample amends for all ;
yes, one moment's enjoyment in heaven, will abundantly recompense you for waiting upon God in the
open face of difficulties.   Believers that would hold
on through all danger, must look more at the crown,
than upon the cross ; more upon the future glory,
than their present misery ; and more upon their encouragements, than upon their discouragements.
This made the Apostle cry out, in all his difficulties
in waiting upon God, *We know that we have a*

*building of God, an house not made with hands,
eternal in the heavens.* He looked for a house that
had foundations, whose builder and maker was God,
and an heavenly country. This also supported
Jesus Christ through all his sufferings : *He endured the cross, despising the shame, and is set down,
&c.*

The sixth Remedy is, solemnly to consider, that
there is not only a reward for keeping the service of
God, but in the present use of it.

Psalm xix. 11.
Great reward.

The service of God and true religion is a present
honor and reward to the righteous, as well as a future glory and immortality. Wisdom's ways are
strewed with roses, and paved with joy that is unspeakable and full of glory, and attended with that
peace that in the present state passeth all understanding to carnal men. The joy, the reward, the
rest, the peace, the content, the smiles, the income
that the saints enjoy in the ways of God, exceed all
the delights of the world, and more than balance all
the difficulties that can attend the faithful performance of them ; yea they are so precious and glorious in their eyes, that they would not exchange them
for ten thousand worlds. Ah! my brethren, if the
work of righteousness be peace, and the effect be

10

quietness and assurance forever, what must the pay-
day be, when Christ shall crown his saints with nev-
er-failing glory and blessedness; and shall say of
them to his Father, "Lo, here am I, and the children which thou hast given me; let them be with
me where I am, to behold my glory."

CHAP. XIV.

THE SECOND DEVICE OF SATAN TO DRAW THE SOUL
FROM HOLY DUTIES, IS BY LEADING SOME TO DRAW
FALSE INFERENCES FROM WHAT CHRIST HAS DONE.

2 PETER ii. 19, 20.
They promise themselves liberty, &c.—Are the ser-
vants of corruption.

OH! saith Satan, do you not know that Christ
has done all for you? Therefore there is nothing
for you to do now, but to believe that he has done
all, and to rejoice in this finished salvation; for he
hath perfectly fulfilled the law, satisfied divine justice,
and pacified divine anger; and you are justified
from all things, from which you never could have
been justified by the law of Moses: and he is now
gone into heaven to prepare a place for you, and to
intercede for you, at the right hand of God. Therefore away with all those legal preachers, who would
bring you into bondage again to works and to duties, since Christ is the end of the law for righteousness to every one that believeth; away with all that
praying, mourning, and hearing and repenting before men for your sins; you do not need these outward services; they are designed for young profes-

sors, and those who cannot believe, and rely upon
Christ, without so many frames and feelings. Ah!
what a world of professors hath Satan deceived with
this device, and drawn them from the use of the
means, under false notions.

The precious Remedies against this device of Satan are these:

First. Carefully to consider, that it is our duty
to love and obey those scriptures that point out our
duty to God, as well as those scriptures that declare
the precious obedience of Christ, &c. &c.

1 CORINTHIANS xv. 58.
Abounding in the work of the Lord.

To dwell as much upon those scriptures that shew
you the duties that Christ requires of you, as upon
those that represent the glorious satisfaction of Christ.
It is a sad and dangerous thing to have two eyes to
behold the dignity and perfection of the doctrines of
grace, and not one to see the honorable paths of
righteousness and peace, to walk therein. I would
look with one eye upon the excellent obedience of
Christ, to raise my heart to love him with the purest
affection, and to rejoice in him with the strongest joy,
and lift up Christ as my Lord above all in the sinner's salvation, and give him all the glory; and with

the other eye I would look upon those services and duties that are required of me as evidence of my being a child of God, and as testimonials of my believing in the merits of Jesus Christ, with a heart unto righteousness. Tertullian saith, " I adore the fulness of the scriptures." Gregory calls the scriptures, the heart and soul of God : and I will say that they are the whole of a Christian.

The second Remedy is, attentively to consider, that the glorious merits, &c. of Christ, are the strongest motives to holy obedience that the scriptures make use of.

2 CORINTHIANS vii. 1.

Having these promises, let us cleanse ourselves, &c.
perfecting holiness in the fear of God.

The great and glorious obedience of Christ should be so far from taking us off from religious services, that it should be the greatest motive and the noblest argument to enforce the performance of them. Jesus Christ hath freed you from all your enemies, from the curse of the law, the predominant and damnatory power of sin, the wrath of God, the sting of death, and the torments of hell. But what is the end and design of Christ in doing all these things for us? Surely it cannot be to free you from all obligation to the law of righteousness and faith; but to constrain you to love, that your hearts may be the more

10*

free, and sweetly engaged in all holy duties. Christ hath therefore broken the devil's yoke from off our necks, that his Father might have better service from our hearts. Ah! sirs, I know no such arguments to move you to a lively and constant performance of divine service, like those that are drawn from the great and glorious things that Christ hath done for you; and if such motives will not win upon you to be diligent and lively in the ways of God, I do believe, that if all the terrors of hell were let loose upon you they could not.

The third Remedy is, seriously to consider, that all the holy prophets, apostles, and saints of old were exceedingly active and lively in the duties of religion.

HEBREWS xii. 1.

Wherefore, seeing we also are compassed about with
so great a cloud of witnesses, let us run, &c.

Those pious souls who believed in Jesus, and had taken rest under the shadow of his wing, were exceedingly active and zealous for the performance of good works; they prayed, praised, and meditated more on God's law than David: the same may I say of Abraham, Isaac, Jacob, Moses, Job, Daniel, and all the prophets. And who more attentive and holy in all conversation and godliness, than the apostles? Have not all those worthies abounded in works of righteousness and peace, to the praise of the free grace of God? Certainly Satan hath got the mastery over such souls that can argue thus: Christ hath done such and such things that are glorious and complete in themselves, and can want nothing in or from us, to render them more acceptable to God; therefore we need not be so much concerned for outward duties, nor trouble our consciences so much about ordinances, for they are no ways essential nor meritorious, for Christ is all and in all to his church. What would the apostles and prophets of our Lord have said unto such? Surely they would blush to look upon such souls, and would turn away from them as sensual men; men not having the spirit of God.

The fourth Remedy is, solemnly to consider, that there can be no true faith in, nor reliance upon Jesus Christ for salvation, without evidences.

1 JOHN iii. 7, 10.
In this the children of God are manifest.

Such persons that do not walk in ways of righteousness and peace, that do not wait upon God in the several appointed duties that God's most holy word points out, cannot have that evidence to their own souls of their acceptance before God, their fellowship and communion with God, and of their blessedness here and happiness hereafter, which those souls have that love and delight in the ways of the Lord. David's daughters were known by their garments of divers colors; so are God's children known by their piety and attachment to the house of God. It is one thing to judge ourselves by our graces, and another thing to rest upon them; for there must be a great difference between declaring ourselves to be the children of God by evidences in fruit, and our meriting by doing. Christianity is not a talking, but a walking with God. To look after holy and heavenly works is the best way to preserve our souls from being deceived and deluded by Satan, or by sudden flashes of joy and comfort, or to a dry notional belief of the gospel; fruits of good works being a more sensible and constant pledge of the Holy Spirit, and a most solemn and clear manifestation of the sons of God, while the contrary is a stubborn evidence of the children of the devil.

The fifth Remedy is, carefully to consider, that saints are not esteemed for the number of duties, but for the manner and end (or design) of them.

GALATIANS v. 25.

If we live in the spirit, let us also walk in the spirit.

There are other choice and glorious ends for the saints performance of good works, than for the justifying of their persons before God, or for their satisfying of the law and justice of God, or for the procuring of pardon for sin, &c. viz. to testify their

justification, to testify their love to God, their sincere
regard to his will ; to testify their deliverance from
the power of sin and the bondage of corruption ; to
evidence the in-dwellings of the spirit, to stop the
mouths of the worst men, and to gladden or rejoice
the souls of the righteous, who were sad. These,
and abundance of other choice and precious ends and
designs, move the children of God to a constant and
lively attendance on the worship of God, and to keep
close to all holy duties commanded by Jesus Christ.
It is a precious truth, and ought never to be forgotten, that duties are to be esteemed not by their acts,
but by their ends ; and the end moves to doing.
The motto of Maximilian is worthy of imitation :
" Keep thyself within the compass, and have an eye
always to the end of thy life and actions." My
brethren, if these considerations will not prevail with
you to wait upon God, I am at a loss to say what
would.

The sixth Remedy is, seriously to consider, that
the true use of the means of grace leads the soul to
rest in Christ.

JOHN vi. 68.

To whom should we go? Thou hast the words of
eternal life.

The exercise of grace in the true use of the duties of religion, is like the star that leads to Christ.

That wisdom which a believer hath from Christ, leads him in the use of all means to centre in the wisdom of Christ: and that love the soul hath from Christ in the means, leads him to rest in his love to Christ; and that righteousness the soul hath from Christ, constrains the soul to confide in his righteousness for justification. True grace is a beam of Christ, and where that is, it will naturally draw the soul to rest alone in Christ on all works and duties. The streams naturally lead to the fountain; the effect to the cause: so a true use of the means of grace doth more forcibly draw the soul to rest in Christ. But temporary grace, restraining grace, and morality, only lead the soul to rest in acts and duties or centre in the creature: such souls have their reward, but not from Christ.

CHAP. XV.

THE THIRD DEVICE OF SATAN TO DRAW THE SOUL
FROM HOLY DUTIES, IS BY REPRESENTING THE PAU-
CITY AND POVERTY OF THOSE THAT WALK IN THEM.

JOHN vii. 47, 48, 49.

Are ye also deceived? Have any of the rulers be-
lieved on him ?

SAITH Satan, look into the world amongst those
who pretend to believe on Christ, and you will be
satisfied that neither the Pharisees, nor rulers, nor
rich, no, nor yet the scribes nor learned men of the
age, have believed on him, nor walked in his ways ;
but this poor, weak, and ignorant few, who are not
to be regarded. If there was any thing noble, profitable, and praise-worthy, you may rest assured
that such great and good men as the Pharisees, and
other wise men, would be found in the duties and
services of the gospel ; and that the ways of religion would be esteemed by the great and more honorable part of mankind. There can be no real
greatness or satisfaction in these ways and practices, that so few and so poor a part of mankind doth
choose to walk in ; and therefore consider, that you
will be singular, and lose all your comforts in life,

if you associate yourselves with the poor, weak and ignorant worshippers of Christ in this odd and new mode of worship: and besides, your grandfathers and great-grandfathers kept at a proper distance from all those weak-headed people; cleave to the mode and manners of your noble ancestors, and let them take their course.

———

The precious Remedies against this device of Satan are these:

First. Deliberately to consider, that though the saints are in general poor, yet they are rich.

LUKE xii. 32.

Fear not little flock, it is your Father's good pleasure to give you the kingdom.

What though the people of God should in general be but few, and poor in this world, yet are they inwardly rich: poor in temporals, but rich in spirituals: the true worth of the saints is inward. The king's daughter is all glorious within. What though they have little in possession, yet have they a glorious kingdom in reversion: though they have little in hand, yet have they much in hope. You count those happy in the world that have much in reversion, though they may not have great things in possession; and can you then count the saints miserable, because they have little in hand, or little in possession, though they have a glorious kingdom in reversion of this? Chrysostom saith, that "places where gold or treasures are hid, are rough, and covered with thorns." Naturalists tell us, that the mountains that are big with gold within, are poor, bare, and ill-looking without. So saints, to the world, look a poor, despicable few, outwardly; but within are big with true riches and honor: and they would not exchange treasures with the world for ten thousand worlds.

The second Remedy is, carefully to consider, that in all ages God hath had some wise, and great, and rich men, who have chosen his ways.

2 KINGS xxiii. 21, 22.
The king commanded all his people to keep the passover.

Although not many wise men, yet some wise men, and though not many mighty, yet some mighty men: and though not many rich men yet some rich men have followed Christ, and been found among the despised few that cleave to the service of God in the open face of difficulties. Abraham, Isaac, Jacob, Job, and several kings, and others, that are recorded in the scriptures, were all righteous men of God, and loved the place were his honor dwelled, and yet were noble and rich in this world's goods.

11

Good nobles, saith one, are like black swans, and thinly scattered in the firmament of a state, even like stars of the first magnitude. And how many have we, among ourselves, whose souls cleave to the Lord, and to his courts, notwithstanding all the poverty of the far greater part of the saints? But call to remembrance the noble army of martyrs, that have swam to the service of God through seas of blood, and who have not counted their lives dear unto them, that they and others might enjoy the holy things of Christ, according to the word and will of God.

The third Remedy is, attentively to consider, that the riches of the poorest saint exceeds the glory of the worldly rich man.

1 CORINTHIANS ii. 9.

Eye hath not seen, nor ear heard, neither hath it entered into the heart of man.

The spiritual treasures and riches of the poorest child of God, infinitely transcend the temporal riches, honor, and glory of all the carnal and wicked men in the world. Spiritual riches satisfy them that possess them: they can retire, and sit down satisfied with the riches of grace and peace that are treasured up in Christ for them, as sons and heirs of God, without the honors and riches of this world. The riches of poor saints are durable treasures; they will bed and board with them, will go to prison, to a

sick bed, to the grave, yea, to heaven with them; for
they can never be parted in life or death, in sickness or in health, in a time of war, or peace, and
in heaven or hell. The spiritual riches of the
saints are their wine, to cheer them; bread to feed
and strengthen them: clothes, to adorn and warm
them; and armor, to protect and defend them. Now
ask yourselves but for one moment, if the treasures
and glory of the world can satisfy the soul of the
possessor, or keep him rich in sickness and in death,
that he shall thirst no more in his soul?

The fourth Remedy is, seriously to consider, that
though the saints comparatively, are few in number,
yet are they without number, and innumerable.

REVELATIONS vii. 9.
Which no man can number, &c.

Although the flock of Christ may, to a carnal
eye appear a little flock, a remnant, a garden en-
closed, a spring shut up, a fountain sealed; though
they are as a summer's gleaning, a handful, a spark
to a flame, a drop to the ocean; and though they
are but as one of a city, and two of a tribe, considered in themselves simply, yet are they an innumerable number, that cannot be numbered. So John
speaking on this subject: "After this I beheld, and
lo! a great multitude, which no man could number,
of all nations, and kindred, and people, and tongues,

stood before the throne, and before the Lamb, clothed with white robes, and palms in their hands."
So saith Matthew: "And I say unto you, that many shall come from the east and west, and shall sit
down with Abraham, Isaac and Jacob, in the king-
kom of heaven." And so Paul: "But ye are
come unto mount Sion, unto the city of the living
God, &c. and to an innumerable company of angels," &c. When Fulgentius saw the nobility of
Rome set mounted in their glory, it mounted his
meditations to the heavenly Jerusalem. What
should the redeemed throng do to us, but mount our
souls?

The fifth Remedy is, solemnly so consider, that
it will be but as a day before these poor despised
saints shall shine brighter than the sun in his glory.

MATTHEW xiii. 43.

Then shall the righteous shine forth as the sun, &c.

It will not be long before you will wish, and cry,
"Oh! that we were now among the poor, mean,
and despised sons of God, who are numbered among
his jewels." It will not be long before these poor feeble saints shall be lifted up on their thrones, to judge
the multitude of the world. Ingo, an ancient king
of the Draves, making a stately feast, appointed his
nobles, at that time pagans, to sit in the hall below,
and commanded certain poor Christians to be

brought up into his presence chamber, to sit with him at his table, to eat and drink of his royal cheer; at which many wondering and murmuring, he said that he accounted the Christians, though never so poor, a greater ornament at his table than his nobles. Just so doth God esteem them. And in that day, oh! how will the great, the rich, the learned and the noble, wish that they had but lived and spent their days with those few, poor, contemptible creatures, in the service of the Lord! Ah! how will this wicked world curse the day that ever they had such low and base thoughts of the poor saints; and that their poverty became a stumbling block to keep them from the ways of God!

The sixth Remedy is, seriously to consider, that a day is approaching, when, in this life, God shall wipe away all reproach from his ways.

REVELATIONS xxi. 24.

The nations shall walk in the light of it, and kings of the earth shall bring their glory unto it.

The Lord hath promised great and glorious days, and that the meek shall inherit the earth : and heaven and earth must and shall pass away, before one jot or tittle of his word shall pass unfulfilled. Ah! poor saints, now some thrust sore at you, others shut you out of doors, others look shy, and turn their backs on you, because of your poverty, and most neglect
11*

and forsake you, because you are few in number in the world. Doth not the scripture say, that the kingdoms of this world must become the kingdoms of our Lord, and that they shall be given to the saints? Hath not God given to Jesus Christ, the heathen, and the uttermost parts of the earth for his possession? Then shall the saints be lifted up above the dunghill, and change poverty for riches, rags for robes, reproaches for crowns, and infamy for glory, even in this world. Who then shall dare to open his mouth to speak a word against the saints, or reproach the ways of God? For the mountain of the Lord's house shall be established in the top of the mountains, and all nations shall flow into it. Saints pray hard for these delightful, these glorious days, that shall roll their reproach away.

CHAP. XVI.

THE FOURTH DEVICE OF SATAN TO DRAW THE SOUL FROM WAITING UPON GOD IN THE USE OF THE MEANS, IS BY CASTING A MULTITUDE OF VAIN THOUGHTS INTO THE MIND.

Ezekiel xxxviii. 10.
Thou shalt think an evil thought.

SATAN, by stirring up a multitude of vain thoughts whilst the soul is seeking of God, or in waiting upon God, in the use of the means, doth so take off our attention, and so cool the affections of many, that they cry, I have no heart to hear, no heart to pray, no heart to read, and no heart to the society of the saints, &c. for Satan doth so closely follow my soul, and cast in my way such a multitude of vain and foolish thoughts concerning God, the world, and my own soul, that I even tremble to think of waiting upon God in any religious service. Oh! the vain thoughts that I feel when at a throne of grace, and on the Lord's day, or at the table of the Lord. What is my service but vanity, and a vexation to my own soul? And I am so distressed and perplexed, that my soul is even weary of holy duties, yea, of my very life. Oh! I am not so raised, ravished, enlar-

ged, and comforted in the ways of God, as I see and
hear others are. Surely there is no person so troubled with vain and wicked thoughts at the time of divine service. If I were a child of God, and the
ways of God a delight to me, sure I could not be so
over-charged with the enemy. Alas! what is there
that Satan will not do to hold us back?

The precious Remedies against this device of Satan are these:

First. Humbly to consider, that our hearts should
be greatly affected with the glory of the Divine Majesty.

2 CHRONICLES vi. 18, 19, 20.
But will God in very deed dwell with men?

In order to have our souls lifted above vain thot's
in our religious exercises, our hearts should be strongly affected with the greatness, holiness, majesty, and
glory of God, before whom we stand, and with
whom our souls do more immediately converse in religious services. Oh! let your souls be greatly concerned with the presence, purity, and majesty of that
God, before whom you stand. A man would be
afraid to play with a feather when in the presence of
a king. When men have poor, low, light, and
flighty thoughts of God, in their drawing near to the

Divine Being, they even tempt the devil to bestir himself, and assist them with a multitude of vain and foolish thoughts, to divert their souls while in waiting upon God. There is nothing can contribute so much to the keeping out of vain thoughts as to look upon God as an omnipotent, omniscient, and omnipresent God; Jehovah, full of all-glorious perfections, and a God, whose infinite purity will not suffer him to behold the least iniquity : these serious considerations and reflections become you, when you come before God, in his worship.

The second Remedy is, carefully to consider, that the soul must be peremptory in waiting upon God.

JOSHUA xxiv. 15.
As for me and my house we will serve the Lord.

A full purpose and resolution to wait on God, notwithstanding all those vain thoughts that wound and trouble the soul. This would be a sweet help against them, saying, " Well, I will pray still, hear still, meditate still, and keep the worship of God still, let my own wicked heart and Satan oppose me never so much with vain thoughts." Many precious souls have by experience found that when their spirits have been peremptory in waiting upon God, Satan hath left them, and hath not tempted them so much as before; when, therefore, Satan finds all these vain thoughts that he tempts the soul with, to keep it back from divine worship, do but vex the soul into greater diligence, carefulness, watchfulness, and a bold peremptoriness in holy and heavenly services, and that the soul loses nothing of its zeal, piety, and devotion, but rather doubles its care, diligence, and earnestness, he ceases to interpose with his trifles and vain thoughts; and thus the worshipper of God cometh off victorious over the enemy.

The third Remedy is, seriously to consider, that vain thoughts, if resisted, are not so sinful as they may be painful.

ROMANS vii. 19.
For the good that I would I do not, &c.

Those vain and trifling thoughts that are cast into our souls when waiting upon God, if they be not cherished and indulged, but abhorred, resisted, and totally disclaimed, then they are not sins upon our souls, though they may be troubles to our minds; they shall not be placed to our account, nor keep mercies and blessings from being enjoyed by us in waiting upon God. When a soul, in uprightness, can look God, as it were, in his face, and say, " Lord, thou knowest that when I would approach near unto thee there is a world of vain thoughts crowding upon me to disturb my soul, weaken my faith, lessen my comforts and spiritual strength, and to pollute thy holy place ; but these are my clog, my burden, my torment, and my hell : oh! do justice upon these ; free me from them, that I may serve thee with more singleness and sweetness of spirit." Vain thoughts pass through the best of hearts, but are lodged and cherished only in the worst : hatred and resistance of our vain thoughts testify the sincerity of our souls to the worship of God.

The fourth Remedy is attentively to consider, that it is a great duty to watch against vain thoughts, as they are inlets to greater evils.

PSALM cxxxix. 23, 24.
Try me and know my thoughts.

Watching against sinful thoughts, resisting, lamenting and complaining of vain thoughts, carries with it the sweetest and the strongest evidence of the truth and power of grace, and the sincerity of your hearts : and it is the readiest and most certain way to be delivered from them. There are many low and carnal considerations that will move a man to watch his words and actions before men ; but to watch the thoughts is something more noble, and springs from a spiritual and internal principle of love to God, a holy fear of God, and a holy care and delight to please. Thoughts are the first born, the blossoms of the soul, the beginning of our strength, whether for good or evil ; and they are the greatest evidence for or against a man that can be. Grace is grown up to a good degree in that soul, where it prevails to the subduing of vain thoughts; and though others should complain that they cannot get rid of them, and it wanteth not their will to overcome them, but they have not the power; still watch, and still make resistance, for help is nigh.

The fifth Remedy is, solemnly to consider the necessity and advantage of having the mind stayed upon God.

Isaiah xxvi. 3.
Thou wilt keep him in perfect peace whose mind is stayed upon thee.

Labor to be more and more filled with the fulness of God, and to be enriched with all spiritual and heavenly things; then both the necessity and advantage of having our thoughts stayed upon God, appears very plain. May I ask, what is the reason that the angels in heaven have not so much as one idle thought? Is it not because that they are so taken up with God, and filled with his fulness, and enriched with spiritual and heavenly objects, and there is not the least room for vain thoughts? The more full a vessel is of wine, the less room there is for water, &c. The more you keep your mind above this world, and stayed upon God, in the contemplation of the divine goodness and beauty, the more shall vain thoughts be put down and spoiled, so as not to be able to lead you captive as heretofore. Oh! then, lay up much of God, of Christ, of precious promises, and choice experience in your hearts; then shall you be less troubled with vain and foolish thoughts that break your peace, and leave you in sad disquiet.

The sixth Remedy is, seriously to consider, that to keep up holy and spiritual affection in the soul, is a proof that we hate vain thoughts.

PSALM cxix. 113.

I hate vain thoughts: but thy law do I love.

The natural affections of man are so placed that they will bring upon your thoughts that will require all that love or hatred you have got, with or against an object. The lawful business of the world, and your calling, will crowd in a multitude of vain thoughts, when in the worship of God; and this, if you are sincere in your soul, you will say, *I hate vain thoughts, but thy law do I love.* But souls that are torn in pieces with cares of this world will be always vexed and tormented with vain thoughts in their approaches to God: they will still come crowding in upon him that knows but little else than the world; so that he will be in the full pursuit of

business in his mind, while his body is in the
house of God, and his eyes beholding the preacher,
nay, while he has the very name of God upon his
tongue. What we most love, we most muse upon; what we most hate, we keep at a greater
distance from. Oh! that you may hate vain thoughts
and love God's law.

CHAP. XVII.

THE FIFTH DEVICE OF SATAN TO DRAW THE SOUL
FROM HOLY DUTIES, IS BY WORKING THE SOUL TO
REST IN THE PERFORMANCE.

EZEKIEL xxxiii. 13.

If he trust to his own righteousness, &c.

THY prayers, hearing, reading, and thy communion, saith Satan, are good and profitable,
both to thyself and others : and what doth the Lord
require of thee, but to do justly, to love mercy, and
to walk humbly with thy God ? And now thou dost
all this, in that thou art very diligent in and at prayer, reading, hearing, and walking with God in the
church, chapel, or meeting, making conscience to
pay thy just concerns, and relieving the poor and
needy : if thou art not right, and in the way to
heaven, who can be so ? Yea, thou seekest God
daily, and delightest to know his ways ; thou forsa-
kest not the ordinances of the Lord, but delightest
in approaching to God, and accustoming thyself to
fasting, &c. Thou mayest surely rest on these good
and excellent performances, as there can be no fear
that thou art not right, and in the highway to heaven ;
for thy prayers and thine alms must go up before

God, and speak for thee against the great day. Thus Satan is for any hand before, either for your neglecting or resting on duties.

———

The precious Remedies against this device of Satan are these:

First.   Patiently to consider, that in our best services there is both weakness and sin.

JOB ix. 20, 21.

If I say I am perfect, it shall also prove me perverse.

Yes, could we but attentively dwell upon the imperfections and weaknesses that do attend our choicest duties, we should soon fall out of love with them, and wonder that an infinite and holy God could bear with patience to hear and see our services. Oh! the spots, the blots, the blemishes, and foul stains that are to be seen upon the face of your fairest duties. When thou hast done all thou canst, thou hast need to close up all with this : "Oh! enter not into judgment with thy servant, O Lord, for the sins and the weaknesses that cleave to my best works." You and I may say with the church, "All our righteousness is as a menstruous cloth." If God should be strict to mark what is done amiss in our purest actions, we are undone ; for whatsoever we do, as of ourselves, is but perfect weakness, and from flesh and blood ; and from such performers there is pride, vain confidence, contempt, neglect of Christ, and robbery of God, in the very best performance: who then can rest on his duties.

The second Remedy is, carefully to consider, that our best duties, of themselves, are neither able to comfort nor to save the soul that trusts in them.

JUDGES x. 14.

Go, and cry unto the gods that you have chosen ; let them save you.

Let your souls dwell a moment or two upon the impotency and inability of any of your holiest services, divinely to comfort, refresh, and bear your souls up from fainting and sinking in the days of adversity and sorrow, when darkness and guilt is upon them, and the Lord shall seem to be withdrawn, and the world shall frown upon you. Can your duties give you peace, and satisfy the soul in such a season of distress, when God shall say to you, (as in the text,) in the days of your calamity, as he did to Israel, " Go and cry unto the gods that you have chosen ; let them save you in the time of your tribulation." Go to your prayers, to your hearing, to your fasting, to your alms, &c. and let them help you, if they can support you, if they can deliver you. Nay, if God doth but withhold the influences of his grace from thee, thy former services will be but poor dry breasts

12*

unto thy soul : then shouldest thou cry out, " Oh, none but Christ ! None but Christ ! Oh ! my prayers are not like Christ : one glimpse of Christ, one smile from Christ, in the days of my trouble, will refresh, restore, and revive my soul again. Return unto thy rest, O my soul."

The third Remedy is, seriously to consider, that the soul is infinitely precious.

PSALM xlix. 8.

For the redemption of the soul is precious.

Seriously consider the worth and excellency of thy immortal soul : it is a jewel of more value than heaven and earth ; and the loss of thy soul is incomparable, irreparable, and irrecoverable : if that be lost, all is lost, and thou art undone forever. It will be no matter to thee at last, whether thy soul perished through the neglect of duties, or for resting on them as thy saviours, if thou dost perish. The true estimate of thy soul may be obtained from the counsels and conduct of God in the great doctrines of redemption and grace, wherein thou mayest learn the dignity and the immortality of thy soul ; the wisdom, love, and good-will of God towards thy soul ; the infinite love, grace, and condescension of the adorable person of the Son of God, Jesus Christ, who clothed himself in flesh to redeem thy soul from death and hell ; the infinite merit of his blood to

pardon thy soul; and the excellency of his righteousness, which alone can justify thy soul; and the
infinite power, grace, and peace of the Holy Ghost,
to sanctify and preserve thy soul from sin, that thou
shouldest live and reign forever with God. Rest
not thy precious soul, therefore, on duties.

The fourth Remedy is, solemnly to consider, that
they who trust and warm themselves with these duties, must, at last, lie down in sorrow.

ISAIAH l. 11.

Behold, all ye that kindle a fire.

Surely the good things we do, become evil things,
if we rest our souls on them; and any duty or duties that we rest upon, will as certainly undo us, and
everlastingly destroy our souls, as the greatest enormities in life : yea, those souls, that after they have
done all, do not look up to Christ, and rest and centre upon him alone, casting all their services at the
footstool of Christ, must lie down in sorrow, and
make their bed in hell ; not that the path of duty is
designed to become a snare to the soul, or that there
can be an evil in the performance of duty : no, no ;
the evil, the snare lies in the heart, and in its resting
upon these to comfort and save the soul as if they
were the bosom of Christ, which is the centre of every pious soul. I love the pipe that conveys the water, but my soul is refreshed with drinking the run-

ning waters in the pipe : so the ordinances of God are pipes conveying spiritual waters ; Christ and his salvation runs through them all ; Christ is the crown of crowns, the glory of glories, the heaven of heavens, and the duty of all duties.

The fifth Remedy is, attentively to consider, that God has provided the soul a resting place.

MATTHEW xi. 28, 29.
Come unto me, &c. I will give you rest.

Let us reflect, with growing pleasure, upon both the necessity and excellency of that resting place which God hath provided for the souls above all others. Jesus Christ is the resting place for every poor, needy, weary, and heavy laden sinner; and there can be no other found under heaven for the precious souls of men to rest upon. His infinite person, his rich and free mercy, his unchangeable love, his pure, glorious, matchless, and spotless righteousness, and his infinitely precious and invaluable blood, are our resting places. Poor soul ! dost thou not see God's hiding place for the laboring soul ? Art thou wandering from mountain to hill, from one duty to another, and here and there taking up thy rest, as was the case with the Jews ? Jeremiah lx. 6. " They have forgotten their resting place." Come, now, let me lead thee to the place where thy soul shall find rest : Christ alone can give thee rest from that law and covenant that commands, but giveth no strength to obey; from that stinging conscience which informs thee to do, but cannot rest satisfied in the deed. Hear, oh! hear my text, speaking rest internal and external, temporal and spiritual, in time and through eternity.

The sixth Remedy is, seriously to consider, that duties are like the manna, appointed to feed the soul in the use of them, but become a curse if trusted to.

Exodus xvi. 20.
It bred worms, and stank.

The grand end and design of this manna was to teach them Christ and his salvation, that they should live upon him, and on his providence : so the glorious end and design of the gospel, and its ordinances, is to lead the soul to Christ. This delicious food, wherewith God fed the Israelites in the desarts of Arabia, was a little grain, white, like hoarfrost, it was round, and in size like coriander seed ; it fell every day, in great quantities, round the camps of the Israelites, for forty years, and fed a million of souls daily : those that gathered much had nothing over, and those that gathered less had no lack or want; nothing of it was to remain until to-morrow, or to be trusted to as food for another day, to lead them to rest in God alone : but Israel disobeyed the voice of the Lord, and treasured up, and rested up-

on having bread for the next day : the Lord was
displeased, and the manna proved a snare, and
stank and bred worms, and was a curse unto them.
So you have the hidden manna, to eat under the gospel, in the camps round about the dwellings of Israel, which shall refresh and feed the thousands and ten
thousands of God's children; but if you rest in
them they shall neither feed nor comfort you.

CHAP. XVIII.

AS SATAN HATH HIS DEVICES TO KEEP THE SOUL
FROM HOLY DUTIES, SO HATH HE HIS DEVICES TO
KEEP THE SOUL IN A SAD AND DOUBTING STATE.
HIS FIRST DEVICE IS BY KEEPING THE SOUL PORING
ON SIN, MORE THAN ON THE SAVIOUR.

Isaiah xxiv. 16.

My leanness, my leanness, wo unto me.

IT is indeed a truth of no small moment to a
Christian, that Satan can never rob a believer of
his crown ; yet such is his malice and envy that he
will leave no stone unturned, no means unattempted
to rob them of their comfort, peace and enjoyment
of Christ, and render their lives a pain, and a burden almost insupportable : and in order to accomplish his design he keeps the believer's eye upon his
sins, unworthiness, short comings, and daily omis-
sions, that he is so taken up with his sinfulness as to
lose sight of Christ ; his eye is so fixed upon the
disease that the remedy cannot be discovered ; yea,
the debt is so mused upon that the surety is forgotten. And thus I fear many spend their days in sorrow and mourning, in sighing and complaining, in
doubting and questioning : surely we have no interest in Christ, our graces are not true, our hopes are

nothing, but like the hypocrite's hope, and all our love and enjoyments are delusions.

———

The precious Remedies against this device of Satan are these:

First. Thankfully to consider, that although Christ hath not freed us from the presence of sin, yet he hath from the (damning) power of it.

Romans viii. 1.
There is therefore now no condemnation.

The weakest believer in Jesus should consider, that though Jesus Christ hath not freed him from the indwelling of sin, yet he hath taken away its damning power and guilt. It is most true, that sin and grace were never born together; neither shall sin and grace die together: yet while a believer breathes in this world, they must live together, they must keep house together, though they live at the farthest distance, and have the greatest hatred for each other: still the believer's enemies are always the strongest and most numerous in his own house. Christ hath not promised to free any believer, in this life, from the presence and sight of sin in his own heart; but he hath promised better things: to keep them from the power, evil and guilt of it, that there should be no condemnation for it. The law cannot condemn a believer, for Christ hath

fulfilled in his stead ; divine justice cannot, for
Christ has died ; sins cannot, for Christ has satisfied, and his blood pardons them ; conscience cannot, for Christ is greater than it, and he will not
condemn, and Satan and the world dare not.

The second Remedy is, seriously to consider,
that although Christ hath not delivered us from the
molesting power of sin, yet he hath freed us from the
masterful reign and dominion of it.

ROMANS vi. 14.
Sin shall not have dominion over you.

Come, thou trembling soul, and consider, that
though thy sins molest and vex, and break thy
peace, that thou canst not think of God, nor go to
God, nor speak with God, as thou wouldst, and
art not able to keep thy worship clean, yet Jesus
has freed thy soul from that lordly authority and
masterful reign over the conscience, that it shall not
have dominion over thee. Though thou canst say
as Bradford did of old, " O Lord, sometimes me-
thinks I feel it so with my heart, as if there was no
difference between me and the wicked," &c. still
say, with another saint, " My sins hurt me not,
if they like me not." Now sin reigns in the soul
when the soul willingly and readily obeys it, and
subjects itself to its commands. The commands of
a king whom we love, are actively and faithfully

13

obeyed : but the commands of a tyrant are unwillingly and slowly obeyed : therefore rejoice, and be exceeding glad, for Jesus Christ has spoiled sin, and cut short its reign.

The third Remedy is, carefully to consider, that the eye of the soul should be kept steadfast upon the promises.

JEREMIAH xxxiii. 8.
I will cleanse, &c. I will pardon, &c.

It is a duty as well as a privilege, to keep one eye upon the promises of remission of sin, as well as the other eye upon the inward operations of sin. This is a most certain truth, that God will graciously pardon those sins to his people, that he will not in this life, fully root out. Paul himself prayed thrice to be delivered from the thorn in the flesh ; yet all that God would do for him was to give him a promise : " My grace is sufficient for thee ; I will graciously pardon that to thee which I will not conquer or root out in thee." Ah ! you lamenting souls that spend your days in sighing and groaning, under the sense and burden of your sins, why do you deal so unkindly with God, and so injuriously with your own souls, as not to cast an eye upon those precious promises of remisssion of sins ?— Hear your God, saying, *I, even I am he that blotteth out thy transgressions to-day and to-morrow, &c.* These promises are like the leaves of myrrh, dropping mercy and spices into the heart of the weakest believer.

The fourth Remedy is, solemnly to consider, that all sins were charged upon Christ, and he hath satisfied for the whole.

2 CORINTHIANS v. 21.
For he hath made him to be sin for us.

Let the humble, let the weeping and the mourning soul know and understand, that all sins were charged to Christ's account by an act of imputation, and not by an act of transgression, as debts, which he hath fully satisfied for; and indeed, were there but one single farthing of that debt unpaid, and standing against us, that Christ should have cleared, by his satisfaction, it could not have been consistent with the divine justice to have accepted any part of the payment, or to admit the surety into heaven, to sit down at the right hand of God, until his saints are all gathered home. But all debts are discharged by Christ's death; we are freed, and he is exalted to glory, and hath taken possession of the kingdom for his people. Yea, all our outward and inward sins were made to meet upon Christ, and he bore them in his own body, upon the tree; and divine justice beheld him the greatest of sinners, by imputation and reputation. Come then, ye laboring souls, and *behold the Lamb of God, that taketh away the sins of the world.*

The fifth Remedy is, Attentively to consider, that the Lord for some great end, suffers the soul to be vexed with sin.

Exodus xxiii. 29, 30.
By little and little will I drive them out.

Say you, why should the Lord suffer my soul to be exercised, troubled, and vexed with the operation of sinful corruptions, when he, by his great power and grace, can so soon deliver me from all my enemies, and that when he knows there is nothing in the world that I would sooner be saved from? I will attempt with reverence, to assign thee some important reasons for the Divine conduct in this : be assured, that it is out of no love or regard to sin, nor anger with the prayers of the saints against it; no, nor yet out of any want of the assistance of sin in the world, to magnify the grace of God. It is the glory of God to bring good out of evil, and to restrain that evil so as to work the good pleasure of his will, against both its own author, nature, and design, and yet so as to be free from the least allowance of it. The reasons are, partly, to keep the soul humble, and low in its own eyes ; to put them upon the use of all the divine

helps or means ; to live more upon Christ for sanctification : to wean them from the world, to teach
them compassion to one another, to make them
heart-sick of their absence from Christ, to lead
them to distinguish between a state of grace and
a state of glory, and to keep them from looking
for it.

The sixth Remedy is, humbly to consider, that
to keep poring upon our sins, and to lose sight of
Christ, is rather a sin than a virtue, (to any soul,)
and calls for repentance.

PSALM xlii. 5, 6.
Why art thou cast down, O my soul, &c.

Believers should, indeed, be sorrowful, and repent of their poring upon sin, and being so distressed with it as to neglect to look at Christ ; because
their discouragements flow from ignorance and unbelief : it springs from their ignorance of the riches,
freeness, fulness, and everlastingness of God's love ;
from their ignorance of the power, glory, sufficien-
cy and efficacy of the death of Christ ; and from
their ignorance of the worth, glory, fulness, large-
ness, and completeness of the righteousness of Jesus
Christ ; and from their ignorance of that real, close,
spiritual, glorious, and inseparable union that is between Christ and their precious souls.   Ah ! did
you heartly believe these precious truths, how would
13*

you grieve, lament, and repent over your sighings, groanings, and discouragements of your sins ; because you have dishonored Christ in looking more upon the wound than upon the physician, and the balm of Gilead.   God never gave a believer a new heart, that it should always lie a bleeding heart with discouragements.

CHAP. XIX.

THE SECOND DEVICE OF SATAN TO KEEP THE SOUL
SAD AND DOUBTING, IS BY A FALSE DEFINITION OF
GRACE.

2 CORINTHIANS iv. 2.
Handling the word of God deceitfully.

SATAN knows, that as a false definition of sin
wrongs the soul one way, so false reasonings of grace
will wrong the soul another way,; and I need only
instance this device in one single grace ; that is,
faith.   Oh! how doth Satan labor, with might and
main, to bring men to make a false definition of faith?
Satan works some persons up so high in their views
and descriptions of faith, as that it is a full assurance
of the love of God to a man's own soul in particular,
and a full persuasion of the pardon of our sins in
general: therefore, saith he, what hast thou to do
with faith ?   It is the full assurance, and thou hast
not got this, therefore thy faith is no faith.   Others
represent faith so low, that it is but a bare belief of
the word of God ; therefore a man need not be so
much concerned for faith.   Philosophers say there
are eight degrees of heat; we can only discern three.
If a man should be defined to be a man only by his

height, length, and breadth, what must be made of
those who differ from this rule? So the grace of
faith: if there is no faith but assurance, and no
believer but such.

———

The precious Remedies against this device of Satan are these:

First. Carefully to consider, that there may be
true faith where there is little or no asurance.

ISAIAH l. 10.

*Who is among you that feareth the Lord, &c. that
walketh in darkness.*

Yea, the sons of God are not only to be known
from their strong assurances, but from their darkness
and distress too; their very distress and pain is a
presumptive proof of the seeds and beginninigs of
the grace of God in their souls, and that they are
already born of God. How many are there repre-
sented in scripture as sitting in darkness, snd having
no light of assurance, unto whom the Lord speaks
as unto his children? It is one thing to have a right
to the kingdom of heaven, and another thing to know
it; it is one thing to be beloved of God, and chosen
and called in Jesus Christ, and another thing for a
man to live in the comfortable enjoyment of it, by
full assurance; it is one thing for God to write a

man's name in the book of life, and another thing
for God to tell a man that his name is written there,
and to say to him, " Rejoice, because thy name is
written in heaven." So then, I say, a man may be
a man of God and of grace, yea, have faith, great
faith, and great grace too, and not have full assurance. The Canaanite woman, in the gospel, had
strong faith, yet no assurance, that we can read of.

The second Remedy is, attentively to consider the
scriptural definition of faith.

JOHN i. 12.

*As many as received him, to them he gave power to
become the sons of God.*

The Lord, the spirit of life and power from Jesus
Christ, knoweth the spirits of men, and what gifts
and measure of grace to give unto them, for the true
use and edification of the church of God ; and hath,
in infinite wisdom and grace, condescended to give
such plain and clear accounts of faith, in its nature,
operation, and effects, that the weakest believer
should not mistake him, nor his description. The
spirit, therefore, defines faith to be a receiving of
Christ, a believing on his name, a cleaving of the
soul unto him, a coming to God through him, and a
resting, staying, and relying of the soul upon him
alone for salvation ; in whom ye also trusted after ye
heard the word of truth, the gospel of your salvation,

in whom also. after ye believed, ye were sealed with that holy spirit of promise.   Ephesians
i. 12, 13. It is safest and sweetest to define as
God defines, both vice and grace ; this is the
only way to settle the soul, and to secure it against
the wiles of men and devils, who keep the soul too
much in a sad and doubting state, from false notions.

The third Remedy is, seriously to consider, that
there may be true faith where there is much doubting.

MATTHEW xiv. 31.
O thou of little faith, wherefore didst thou doubt.

Who, that reflects but for a moment on these words
of our Lord to Peter, and considers the apostle himself, but must be led to acknowledge, that, from the
word of God, it appears self-evident, that persons
may be possessed of true and divine faith, who, nevertheless, are in a sad and doubting state ?   In the
case of the disciples, Matthew xvi. 8. "O ye of little
faith, why reason ye among yourselves?"   Jesus
seemeth to commend their faith in one view, and to
condemn their doubts in another, which plainly supposeth the presence of both in the soul.   Doubting,
therefore, though it be quite contrary to faith, yet it
will by no means conclude a man to have no faith at
all, but only a little faith at that season, and in that

circumstance. Peter, by his saying " if it be thou," shewed some marks of weakness in his faith; but when he could say, " bid me come unto thee on the water," it seemed a degree of stronger faith; but afterwards he feared: the wind and seas began to rise, and losing sight of Jesus, as God of the seas, he began to sink. Thus Peter is a pattern to both weak and strong faith; to weak faith, not to be dejected; to strong faith, not to be presumptive.

The fourth Remedy is, diligently to consider, that assurance is not faith, but the fruit and effect of faith.

HEBREWS xi. 1.

Faith is the substance of things hoped for, the evidence of things not seen.

No man will say, that the effect is the cause, nor that the fruit is the root of the tree; but the cause must be in the effect, and the root in the fruit; and yet the cause cannot be the effect, nor the root the fruit: therefore, as the effect flows from the cause, the fruit from the root, and the stream from the fountain, so doth this assurance flow from faith. Now no man can have assurance, and be fully persuaded of his salvation in Jesus Christ, until his soul be closely united to Christ, nor until he be ingrafted into Christ; and it is very plain that a man cannot be thus ingrafted into Christ, till he hath faith in him as the Son of God : and he must first be ingrafted into Christ by faith, before he can have a full assurance of his salvation ; which evidently shews that assurance is not faith, but rather the effect and fruit of saving faith in Jesus Christ : therefore, when Satan would attempt to embarrass your souls by a false description of faith, by saying, you cannot be a believer in Jesus unless you have a full assurance of faith, tell him, that you can rest your soul and your salvation on Christ alone.

The fifth Remedy is, solemnly to consider, that assurance may be lost, but true faith cannot.

PSALM li. 12.
Restore unto me the joy of thy salvation, and uphold me with thy free spirit.

Though assurance be a precious and a sweet flower in the garden of the saints, and to them is infinitely more sweet and delightful than all outward comforts and contents, yet it is but a flower, and subject to fade away and die, leaving the soul to mourn the loss of its beauty and preciousness in its experience. Doth not David sufficiently indicate this truth in the above cited passage ? What joy doth he intend, but the joy of assurance, which he had eminently enjoyed, but which, through the entrance of sin, was now lost, and gone far from him ? Yet his faith re-

mained active: and this text is the prayer of faith,
struggling for victory over those clouds and sorrows
that sin had brought upon him: therefore it appears
evident that assurance of our salvation, and pardon
of sin, doth primarily arise from the witness of the
spirit of God within a man, as a free spirit, that up-
holds the joy of the heart, and that this freedom and
joy of the soul may be both obstructed and lost;
yet faith cannot be lost, though brought to a low
ebb.

The sixth Remedy is, deliberately to consider,
that a man must first have faith, and no small degree of it, before he can have assurance.

2 PETER i. 1.

Like precious faith with us.

A man must first be saved before he can be assured of his salvation, for he cannot be assured of that
which is not; he must first have experience of saving faith, before he can be said to be saved by
faith, for he cannot be saved by that which he hath
not: therefore, I say, that a man must first have faith,
and no small degree of it neither, before he can have
assurance: this will evidence that assurance is not
faith, and that a child of God may be satisfied that
he is indeed a child born of God, although he doth
not enjoy a full assurance; but still it doth not hence
follow, that the saints of God should neglect and dis-

14

regard assurance, because that they may be safe without it; no, by no means; neither can I suppose, for a moment, that true faith in the soul can lead the saints to take satisfaction in any thing short of that which has a tendency to enliven and enrich the growth, power, and the fruits of faith in them who are the saved and the called of God, according to his purpose.

CHAP. XX.

THE THIRD DEVICE THAT SATAN HATH TO KEEP THE
SOUL IN A SAD AND DOUBTING CONDITION, IS BY
SUGGESTING TO IT, THAT ITS GRACES ARE NOT TRUE
BUT FALSE AND COUNTERFEIT GRACES.

ACTS vii. 21.

For thy heart is not right in the sight of God.

SAITH Satan, all is not gold that glitters, all is
not free grace that you call grace; and that which you
call faith, is but a fancy; that which you take for
zeal, is but natural heat and passion; and that
which you esteem as divine light in the soul, is but
common light of reason and understanding in man,
and all what thousands have attained to, who are
now in hell. Satan doth not labor more mightily
to persuade hypocrites that their graces are true
and just when they are counterfeit, than he doth
to persuade precious. souls that their graces are
false and counterfeit, when indeed he knows they
are true, and such as will abide the fire of his temptations. Although I must confess to thee, O Satan!
that many a fair flower may grow out of a vile and
offensive root, so many sweet dispositions and lovely
actions may be found amongst men, where there is only the evil and corrupt root of nature reigning: not-

withstanding, this shall not constitute the graces of the saints to be only counterfeit graces.

———————

The precious Remedies against this device of Satan are these:

First. Seriously to consider, that grace is taken in different senses in scripture.

ROMANS v. 15.
The grace of **God**, *and the gift by grace.*

The word of grace is sometimes taken for the gracious good will and favor of God, whereby he is pleased of his own free love and grace to choose and accept of sinners in Christ, for his own people, and in time to bring them forth as vessels to his own glory : this some call the first grace, because it is the fountain of all other graces, and springs from thence ; and it is therefore called grace, because it makes a man gracious and acceptable to God ; but this grace is only in God. Grace is also taken for the gifts of grace ; and these are of two sorts, common or special.— Some gifts of grace are common to believers and hypocrites ; such are the gifts of knowledge, gifts of tongues, gifts of prayer, &c. and some are special gifts and graces ; and these are proper and peculiar to the saints only ; as faith, humility, meekness, love, patience and delight in God, in an holy and heavenly fellowship and communion with God, and in meditation ; therefore let Satan be resisted steadfastly in the faith, and you shall try a true and false faith.

The second Remedy is wisely to consider the difference between renewing grace and restraining grace.

2 CORINTHIANS ix. 13, 14.
The exceeding grace of God in you.

Renewing grace makes a man all-glorious within and without ; true grace makes the understanding glorious, the will glorious, the affections glorious, and the conscience glorious, yea, it casts a general glory upon all the noble powers of the soul ; and as it makes the soul glorious within, so it makes the outside glorious; it makes men look gloriously, and act gloriously : so that vain men are forced to say, these are they that have seen Jesus ; because they see that all is gloriously made anew. God not only giveth grace to the soul, but he wills that that grace should be made appear to be glorious grace. Purity, preciousness, and holiness are stamped upon every grace of the spirit; but it is not so with restraining grace. A lion, though in a grate, is a lion still ; for he retains his lion-like nature : so temporary graces restrain many men from vice, but do not change and turn their hearts. A new creation, new Adam, new covenant, new paradise, new Lord, new law, new heart, and new nature, all go together.

The third Remedy is, carefully to consider, that divine grace has more sweet and powerful motives to holiness than restraining grace can produce.

2 CORINTHIANS i. 12.

By the grace of God we have had our conversation in the world.

Saving, sanctifying, and renewing grace move the soul of the possessor to spiritual duties, from spiritual and intrinsical motives, from a sense of the divine love and favor which constrains the soul to wait upon God, and to act for God: and the sense of the excellency and sweetness of communion with God, and the choice and precious discoveries that the soul has formerly had of the beauty, glory, and perfections of God, whilst in his service. The pleasant looks, the gracious words, the blessed and endearing epistles of love, the gracious kisses, and sweet and heavenly embraces that the gracious soul hath had from Christ in his service, do move him so powerfully in holy duties, that the soul may be said to be in its divine element. But restraining grace only puts men upon religious duties, from external motives: from the care of the creature, the eye of the world, the rewards of the creature and the obtaining of a good name amongst the professions of the day; so that all that such persons can enjoy in the habits of religious duties, is the gratification of that vain glory and carnal confidence which they receive from men.

The fourth Remedy is, diligently to consider, that true grace leads the soul to be more careful and fearful of the evils of the human heart than of any other enemy.

HEBREWS iii. 12.
Lest there be in any of you an evil heart of unbelief.

The gracious soul is a conscious soul: and no enemy can attack the soul so effectually as the evils of the heart. Grace teaches a man to be more careful and fearful of his own heart, than of all the world besides; grace aids the soul to view all its deceits and wiles, and so assist in the studious inquiry after its evils, that the soul is in full exercise of seeking information, sitting in examination and watchings over an evil heart. But restraining grace doth not find any such thing, and can see no cause for such complaints to be made against the human heart: as for their parts they find, that through the grace of God, and their moral virtues, they can always keep themselves from a multitude that follow evil: and if they are but freed from outward vice and wickedness, they fear nothing else, because they are living strangers to God and to themselves, in the divine life.

The fifth Remedy is, attentively to consider, that true grace enables the soul to prefer the cross of Christ to all temporal glory.

GALATIANS vi. 14.
God forbid that I should glory, save in the cross, &c.

True grace will enable a man to step over the earthly crown to take up Christ's cross : to esteem the cross of Christ above the glory of the world. It was this that enabled Abraham, Moses, and Daniel, with that noble cloud of witnesses in Hebrews xi. so joyfully to take up the cross, and follow Christ.   Godfrey of Boulogne, first king of Jerusalem, refused to be crowned with a crown of gold, saying that it did not become a Christian there to wear a crown of gold, where Christ had worn a crown of thorns.   Oh ! but temporary grace cannot work the soul to prefer Christ's cross above the world's crown ; but when these two meet, a temporary Christian will step over Christ's cross to take up the world. *Demas hath forsaken us to embrace the present world.*   So the young man in the gospel had many things in him that appeared good, and like special graces, but when Christ puts the matter to a near and close trial, and proposeth

the cross, he turns his back upon Christ. God
brings not a pair of scales to weigh our graces, but
a touch stone to try them. How few are of Je-
rome's mind, that had rather have Paul's coat, with
his heavenly graces, than the purple robes of kings,
with their kingdoms.

The sixth Remedy is, solemnly to consider, that
divine grace enables the pious soul to sit down satisfied with the enjoyment of Christ.

PHILLIPIANS iii. 7, 8.

*I count all things but loss, for the excellency of the
knowledge of Christ Jesus, &c.*

The knowledge and enjoyment of Christ, without
honor, will satisfy the soul of a saint ; the enjoyment
of Christ without riches, the enjoyment of Christ
without pleasures, and the enjoyment of Christ without the smiles of the world, can satisfy the souls of
them that believe in Jesus. Christ is all my riches,
honor, glory, wealth, health, and friends ; he reigns,
conquers, and triumphs over all. Christ is the pot
of manna, the cruise of oil, and the ocean of all
comfort, content, and satisfaction: he that hath
Christ, wants nothing ; but he that wants him, wants
every thing, and enjoys nothing. Oh ! restraining
grace puts up with this world without Christ. He
is good to temporary believers when honors, riches,
pleasures, and creature's smiles are found in the cross;

but how seldom doth this take place, if ever ? What a multitude of shining professors are there in the world, that cannot rest satisfied and contented under the want of this or the other outward comfort and delight? Lambert cried out, in the flames, "None but Christ! none but Christ!" Believing souls say there is nothing either good or great but Christ.

CHAP. XXI.

THE FOURTH DEVICE OF SATAN TO KEEP THE SOUL IN A SAD AND DOUBTING STATE, IS BY REPRESENT-ING THE PERSON TO BE IN A LOST AND RUINOUS CONDITION, BECAUSE HE HATH LOST HIS FIRST LOVE.

REVELATIONS ii. 4.

I have somewhat against thee because thou hast lost thy first love.

SURELY, saith Satan, thou art in a dangerous state ; and there can be no good thing found in thee towards the Lord, because thou canst not joy and rejoice in Christ as in the days of thy first love, when thou wentest after Christ in a land that was not seen. Yea, saith Satan, thou knowest the time was when thy heart was much carried out in holy ecstacy and triumphs, when thou couldest have died for his name, for thy cup ran over, and thy soul longed to be gone : but now the scene is changed ; thy love is cold, thy soul dead and barren, and all thy joys and ecstacies are departed from thy soul, and nothing re-mains but a round of dry and formal duties : see therefore, that thy state cannot be good ; thou art deceiving thyself to imagine that there ever was any thing good in thee, for surely if it had been good, and a work of God, thy love and joy would have remained the same. Oh, thou devil! I feel thy rage and thy malice against the souls of men in my own experience; and it may be there are many precious souls groaning under this device of Satan: let me then lead you to some precious remedies.

———

The precious Remedies against this device of Satan are these:

First. Seriously to consider, that the christian may be full of holy affections when he is empty of divine consolations.

PSALM lxiii. 1, 2.
My soul thirsteth for thee, &c.

The loss of spiritual comfort is common to the people of God; and there may be, and often is, true grace, yea, much grace, where there is not a drop of comfort, nor a dram of divine consolation in the soul. Comfort is not the being of a child of God, but the well-being, or the vigorous enjoyments of a Christian in the divine life: God hath not so linked these two choice lovers together, but that they may be put asunder. That wisdom that is from above will never work a man to reason thus: I have no comfort, therefore I have no grace; I have lost that joy that once I had, therefore my condition is not good, was never good; the light of the divine coun-

tenance is gone from me, therefore the Lord is departed, and left me a prey to my own evil heart, &c.
But it will enable a man to reason thus : Though
my comfort is gone, yet God, who is the infinite
source of all my joy and consolation, abides ; though
my pleasant frames be lost, yet the seeds of grace
remain. Spiritual joy is a sun that is often clouded,
though it be precious to walk in the clear shinings
thereof. The joys of the best men upon earth are as
glass, bright and brittle, and ever more in danger of
breaking.

The second Remedy is, solemnly to consider, that
when comfort is departed from the soul, the precious union with Christ still remains the same.

MALACHI ii. 14, 15, 16.

*The Lord, the God of Israel saith, he hateth put-
ting away.*

Consider that the precious things that thou still enjoyest, are far better than the joys and comforts that
thou hast lost. Thy union with Christ, thy communion, thy sonship, thy saintship, and thy heirship, that
thou still enjoyest by Christ, are far better than all
the comforts thou hast lost. Reason thou, therefore,
thus within thyself, and say, " Well, Satan, I acknowledge that, through my foolishness and sins, I
have lost my first love and comforts ; yet I am a son,
an heir, and a saint, though comfortless ; though the

15

bag of silver be lost, yet the box of jewels is safe: Christ is safe, pardon is safe, righteousness is safe, union is safe, communion is safe, and heaven and eternal comfort and joy are safe, though my present and temporary comforts are changed." The least of those jewels is more precious and noble than all the comforts thou hast tasted in thy youth. Let this be a consolation, a cordial to comfort thee, a star to lead thee, and a staff to support thee in the way, that however thy joys come and go, and frequently leave thee comfortless, yet the cabinet of jewels is safe from thieves and robbers.

The third Remedy is, attentively to consider, that the causes of joy and comforts are not always the same.

PSALM cxxxvii. 1, 2, 3, 4.
How shall we sing the Lord's song in a strange
land.

Thy former joy and comfort might spring from the witness of the spirit, he bearing witness to thy soul, that thy heart and nature were changed, thy sins pardoned, thy soul justified, and thyself now reconciled to God. But now the spirit may, upon some special occasions, bear witness to thy soul, that the heart of God is dearly set upon thee, and that he loves thee with an everlasting love, &c. and yet thou mayest not enjoy so clear a testimony all the days of thy life again. Or it may be that thy former joy

and comfort did spring from the newness and sudden
surprise of the change that grace had wrought upon
thy soul: for a man to have God's anger and frowns
turned into smiles, his hatred into love, his hell into
a heaven, must cause his soul to leap for joy. It
cannot but make his heart glad to see Satan accu-
sing, his own mind condemning, God frowning upon
him, the gates of heaven barred against him, and
nothing but the infernal pit appearing for him : now
in such an hour, with such feelings, for Christ to
step into the soul, and say, "Fear not, I am thy
salvation, I will help thee, yea, I will uphold, &c."
Oh! what tongue can express this joy.

The fourth Remedy is, carefully to consider, that
the case of the comfortless soul is not singular, but
common to all the saints.

1 PETER v. 8, 9.
The same afflictions are accomplished in your brethren
that are in the world.

Thy condition is no other than what hath been
the state and experience of the saints of old; for
those precious souls whose names were written upon
the heart of Christ, and who are now at rest in the
bosom of Christ, were once and again in their day,
sighing and grieving for the loss of those comforts and
sensible consolations of their souls, as thou dost in
this day of thy sorrow. Mark the scriptures, and

you will hear them one day praising, exulting, joying, and rejoicing in the God of their salvation, and venturing to predict that their mountain stands so strong it shall never be moved : but the Lord hides his face, and withdraws the comforts from the soul, then all is darkness and distress; then the days of their weeping and mourning come upon them. The spirit has not promised you a feast every day; you must not expect to wear the wedding robes every day in the week ; no. it is pretty well if you get them on upon royal days, and when you see the king in his beauty. Therefore remember, that although the first joy, the great joy of your deliverance may be abated, yet your life is the same ; precious with God. Joy, therefore, in God alone.

The fifth Remedy is, seriously to consider, that God will restore and make up the comforts of his people.

ISAIAH lvii. 18.

I have seen his ways, and will heal him, &c. and restore comforts unto him.

Though thy sun, for the present, be clouded, yet he that rides upon the clouds shall scatter those interposing clouds, and cause the sun to shine and warm thy heart, as in former days. God takes away a little comfort, that he may make room in the soul for a greater degree of comfort. What though thy candle be gone out, yet God shall light it again, and

cause it to burn brighter, than ever. The Psalmist
saith, " Thou which hast shewed me great and sore
troubles shalt quicken me again, and shalt bring me
up again, from the depths of the earth. Thou shalt
increase my greatness, and comfort me on every
side." Psalm lxxi. 20, 21. Hudson the martyr, being deserted at the time of his suffering, went from
under the stake, and prayed earnestly, and the Lord
heard and enlivened his soul, and he suffered valiant-
ly. Mr. Glover, when he was led from prison,
was in great darkness, but when he saw the stake,
cried out, to his friend, "He is come! He is come!"
Meaning the spirit, the comforter promised by Jesus
Christ to all his saints. Bear up sweetly, O precious
soul! He will come, he will come to thee.

The sixth Remedy is, solemnly to consider, that
as all sin is hateful to God, so are all those things
that rob the soul of spiritual comforts hateful to the
children of God.

ROMANS vii. 15.
But what I hate that do I.

The universal conflicts of the saints, both with
great and small, with internal and external sins and
infirmities, confirm the important truth of Peter's reply to his Lord on the nature and evidence of his
love to Jesus after that shameful denial of him before
men. Lord, thou knowest all things; thou know-

15*

est that I love thee : my love is abated, and my zeal is cooler than when I first loved thee ; but thou knowest all things, and that I earnestly love thee still, although it is not with me as in days past. The fool looks upon one sin, and sees that that cast down Noah, the most righteous man in the world; and he looks upon another sin, and sees that that cast down Abraham, the greatest beliver in the world ; and he looks upon another sin, and sees that that cast down Moses, the meekest man in the world; and he looks upon another sin, and finds that that cast down Sampson, the strongest man in the world, &c. therefore he concludes that there is no rest nor comfort for a comfortless man, but in the Lord alone, and that by these things the soul is brought off from self, duties, and creatures, to lean upon the cross.

CHAP. XXII.

THE FIFTH DEVICE OF SATAN TO KEEP THE SOUL IN
A SAD AND DOUBTING STATE, IS BY REPRESENTING
THE MANY RELAPSES INTO THE SAME SIN, AND THE
BACKSLIDINGS OF THE SOUL, AS TOO HEINOUS TO BE
FORGIVEN.

PSALM iii. 2.

There is no help for him in God.

OH! saith Satan, thy heart cannot be sincere
and right with God, for thou hast often relapsed into the same sin, which formerly thou didst pursue
with particular sorrow, grief, and shame, and with
mighty prayer and watchfulness; but now thou art,
after all, overcome, and hast backsliden again into
foul sins: surely thou art not a saint nor a child of
God! How canst thou think that the Lord can accept thee, and eternally save such a one as thou art,
who complainest against sin, and yet falls again into
the very same sin? Thy prayers, sighings, and
repentings are not good, nor can they spring from
a true sorrow and hatred of sin, or love to Jesus
Christ and his commandments; therefore deceive
not thyself and others, for thou art in a bad state,
and thy religion only serves to make thee miserable
here and hereafter too: for there can be no forgiveness for backsliding and turning again to folly, so

many times as thou hast. Thus Satan gets the advantage over our soul, and holds us in a sad and doubting condition all our days.

The precious Remedies against this device of Satan are these:

First. Seriously to consider, that the scriptures are particularly clear and encouraging on this point.

Hosea xiv. 4.
I will heal their backslidings, I will love them freely.

That the gracious word of God doth clearly evidence a possibility of the saints falling into the same sin again, notwithstanding their former sorrow, cannot be denied; and it is a mercy, and matter of eternal thankfulness, that the wisdom and goodness of God has so fully revealed it in the scripture, that the returning soul might have hope.—Come, hear now, the declarations of the Lord our God: "Turn, O backsliding Israel, saith the Lord, for I am married unto you. Return, thou backsliding Israel, saith the Lord, and I will not cause mine anger to fall upon you; for I am merciful, saith the Lord. How shall I give thee up, Ephraim? How shall I deliver thee, Israel? My heart is turned within me, my repentings are kindled together." Hosea xi. 7, 8, &c. &c. When a soldier boasted too much of a great scar in his forehead, before Augustus Cæsar, he asked him, if he did not get that wound by looking back as he fled? So, alas! the christian is often wounded by looking back, and fleeing before sin, rather than fleeing upon it, to cut it off forever.

The second Remedy is, solemnly to consider that the seeds of sin are both deep and strong, while grace and repentance are but weak and feeble, there being no particular promise from God to keep the soul from a possibility of a relapse.

GALATIANS vi. 1.

Considering thyself, lest thou also be tempted.

I cannot make it a wonder and an astonishment beyond comparison, if a child of God should fall into the same error as before, when we consider that repentance though never so sincere and sound, is but weak, and an act of a feeble man or woman; and the repeated cautions and admonitions of the spirit of God in the scriptures on this head, together with those noble and gracious addresses of the Lord to backsliding souls; neither can I find any engagements on the Lord's side to keep any of his saints from the possibility of sin: after their conversion, the power, the reign, and the damning authority and guilt of sin is destroyed, and promise made that it shall never have dominion over them.

as before, in its unconquered and absolute power; still there is no promise to insure the soul of an impossibility of sin in the seeds thereof never putting up head and requiring the pruning knife. This is not intended to keep the soul in bondage, nor to encourage the backslider to go on in relapses.

The third Remedy is, carefully to consider, that the soul too often relapses into infirmities or weaknesses, as well as into outward sins.

HEBREWS iv. 15.

Touched with the feeling of our infirmities.

As I dare not deny relapses into enormities, or outward sins, so neither can I deny that saints relapse into infirmities. It is not usual with the Lord to leave his people frequently to fall into enormities ; for his spirit and grace, his smiles and frowns, his word and rod, do preserve them from a compliance : yet you may find that saints too frequently do relapse into infirmities. I mean, by relapses into infirmities, the repeated giving way to idle words, passion, vain thoughts, and other unprofitable talk and works. It is indeed a truth of great moment, that saints do strive against those sins, and complain of them before the Lord, and frequently go weeping to the altar of the Lord on account of those sins, crying out of their foolishness, in the disquietude of their souls. But the Lord who is infinite in compassion, is graciously pleased to look down, and to place underneath the soul his everlasting arms, and so support the weeping saint from perishing under the weight of his infirmities, and melt the heart with his loving kindness.

The fourth Remedy is, attentively to consider, that there are both involuntary relapses and voluntary ones.

HOSEA xi. 12.

Ephraim compasseth me about with lies, &c. but Judah yet ruleth with God, and is faithful, &c.

Involuntary relapses are when the resolution and bent of the heart is against sin, when the soul strives with all its might against sin, by prayers, tears, sighs, and groans, and yet cannot find victory, or strength sufficient to hold out, but through weakness is forced to fall back; and so sin takes the advantage of the soul. Though involuntary sins and infirmities are sufficient causes of humiliation, yet they should not discourage nor deject us, for God will surely pardon. Voluntary relapses are, when the soul takes an active part with the tempter and the snare, to enslave and indulge the soul in the commission of the sin, and there is a delight to go back into folly, and a freedom in the act. May I not say there is a great and an essential difference between a sheep that, through much weakness falls into the mire, and a swine that naturally delights to wallow in the mire? How very consistent this comparison with the word of God, 2 Peter ii. 22. Then let saints lift up their heads, and be not discouraged, for God is with them to deliver.

The fifth remedy is, diligently to consider, that neither the greatest sorrow for sin, nor the choicest discoveries of God (manifested) to the soul, can be an absolute freedom from the in-being of sin.

2 CORINTHIANS xii. 2, 7.

A messenger of Satan to buffet me.

There can be no such power or infinite virtue in the deepest sorrow of soul under sin, as to insure that heart that the least seed of the old corruption shall not rise any more ; nor so much essential purity and grace communicated unto the soul, under the gracious discoveries of God's love and favor to the soul, as that the person should venture to assert himself absolutely clear and free from the least returning of his nature to sin and sinful infirmities. Those gracious manifestations of God to the soul, are glorious seasons to the people of God ; but they do not always abide in their power and sweetness upon the heart, nor can the most elevated station deliver you from the danger of repeated relapses. Peter, James and John were exalted to the mount of Christ's transfiguration, and saw his glory, but did that prevent them from infirmities, and natural actings of their unsanctified part? No; they slept and slumbered so much, as to lose the noblest sight on earth. Luke ix. 28, 37. Alas! we find that the greatest saint is but weakness when left.

The sixth Remedy is, seriously to consider, that the whole frame of a believer's soul is against sin, and the conflict with the saint is universal through the whole frame of both soul and body.

HEBREWS xii. 4.

Resisting unto blood, striving against sin.

The whole frame of a believer's soul is against sin in all its natures, operations and effects; the understanding, will, and affections, and all the powers and faculties of the soul are in arms against sin, and the conflict is universal with the least as well as with the greatest, the most profitable and the most pleasing, as well as the less pleasing and profitable sin, and the relapses into sin; and this conflict is maintained by spiritual weapons and arguments, such as the soul draws from the love of God, the honor of God, the person of Christ, his blood, his righteousness, and his glory; the Holy Spirit, his seal, his earnest, his witness, and his comforting influences to the soul, &c.; and further, this conflict of the saints against sin is in the very same facul-

16

ties and powers of the soul, is the unregenerate part against the regenerate part, in all parts of the soul ; as judgment against judgment, will against will, and the affections against the affections, &c. So then, though Christ hath given sin its death stroke, yet it will die but a lingering death, and the Christian must resist unto blood, striving against sin.

CHAP. XXIII.

THE SIXTH DEVICE OF SATAN TO KEEP THE SOUL IN
A SAD AND DOUBTING CONDITION, IS BY PERSUA-
DING THE SOUL THAT IT CANNOT BE IN A GOOD
STATE, BECAUSE IT IS VEXED WITH SO MANY TEMP-
TATIONS.

I THESSALONIANS iii. 5.

*The tempter have tempted you, and our labor be in
vain.*

SATAN saith, thy state and thy heart cannot be
good, nor right in the sight of God, because thou
art continually followed, vexed, and tormented with
so many awful temptations. Satan's method is first
to vex and weary the soul with his devices and temptations, and then to tempt and torment the soul, that
it is an impossibility for any good to be found in
him, when so many evil desires, and vain and foolish
reasonings are continually pouring themselves into
the mind. Now, saith Satan, if God loved you with
the same love that he doth his own children, then, no
doubt, he would keep you from those temptations
which break your peace and dishonor God. For
what blasphemous thoughts against the person, perfections, and government of God, do you find work-

ing within your bosom? And what evil and dishonoring thoughts spring up within you against the bible, which tempt you to believe that it is not the word of God &c. Satan tempted Job to be even weary of his life. Job x. 1. "My soul is weary of my life." Thus Satan, by this stratagem, keeps many precious souls in a sad and doubting state for many years.

———

The precious Remedies against this device of Satan are these :

First. Seriously to consider, that those saints that enjoy most of the divine presence are most vexed with Satan.

HEBREWS ii. 18.

He being tempted is able to succor them that are tempted.

Let us consider that those saints that have been best and most beloved of God, and have enjoyed most of the divine presence in this life, have been the most tempted and vexed by Satan. Christ himself was the most near, most dear, most excellent, and the most innocent person upon earth, and yet no one was ever so much tempted as Christ. Abraham was a friend of God, and the father of the faithful, yet he was greatly tempted. David was dearly beloved of God, and a man after his own heart, and loved of God, and a man after his own heart, and

yet loaded with temptations. Job was a perfect and an upright man, and greatly praised by the Lord, yet much tempted by the devil. Peter was greatly beloved and prized by Christ, yet much vexed with temptations. Paul had peculiar honors conferred upon him by the Lord, and yet Satan buffeted him continually, &c. Now if those that were so really, so gloriously, and so eminently beloved of God, have been tempted each one in his day by Satan, with such inveterate malice and implacable wrath, let no saint be discouraged, in that he is tempted, to believe he is not beloved of God, because he is vexed with Satan.

The second Remedy is, carefully to consider, that all the temptations that befal the saints do in the end work together for their good.

JAMES i. 2.

Count it all joy when ye fall into divers temptations.

Temptations are God's seminaries and schools, where he teaches the choice lessons of experience and grace ; a seminary, where he makes a preacher of the gospel ; a school, where the Lord teaches the noble and powerful doctrines of humility, compassion, and patience with one another. Ah ! the choice experiences that saints get of the power of God supporting, the wisdom of God directing, and the love of God encouraging them under every temp-

16*

tation. Luther said, " There be three things that
make a preacher ; meditation, prayer, and temptation." Herein God opens the human heart to a
more full and clear discovery of its evils ; herein sin
appears exceeding sinful ; and herein the vanity and
emptiness of all created good is exposed. And thus
the issue of all temptations shall be the real good and
advantage of the saints in the end ; for God is able
to make all things work together for good unto them
that love God, so that out of the eater shall come
forth meat, and out of the strong shall come forth
sweetness; and from those temptations saints learn
how to put on and handle their spiritual weapons,
and to stand fast like valiant men, in the faith.

The third Remedy is, solemnly to consider, that
no temptation can harm the soul if resisted.

REVELATIONS iii. 10.
*Because thou hast kept the word of my patience, I
also will keep thee from the hour of temptation.*

There is no temptation that can harm you, so long
as resistance is made against it. 'Tis not Satan's
tempting, but your assenting ; 'tis not his enticing,
but your yielding, that can harm you. If the soul,
when tempted, resists, and, with Christ, saith to the
temptation, " Get thee behind me, Satan ;" and,
with a certain young convert, say, " Begone, Satan,
for I am not the man that I was ;" or as Luther

counsels all men to answer all temptations with these words: "I am a Christian." If a man's temptations be his greatest affliction, then is the temptation no sin upon his soul, though it be a trouble upon his mind. When your souls can, in the strictest sense of the words, address the Lord, and say, "Ah! Lord, thou knowest that I have many outward troubles upon me, and that I have lost many mercies, yea, the most dear and lovely mercies in the world, and yet all these mercies, crosses, and losses do not make so many wounds in my soul, nor cause me to fetch such heavy sighs from my heart, nor tears from my eyes, as those temptations do that Satan follows up my soul with." When it is thus with you, then the temptations of Satan are the soul's troubles, but not the soul's sins; therefore you have reason rather to rejoice, and be exceeding glad, as the temptation cannot harm you, although it should vex you.

The fourth Remedy is, attentively to consider, that Satan is a malicious and envious enemy to the soul; and that as his names are, so is he.

1 PETER v. 8.
Adversary, the devil as a roaring lion.

The scriptures have wonderfully assisted the saints to find out the malice and hatred of Satan against them, by those names and characters given to him, which are all names and characters of enmity. He is called the accuser, because he accuseth the saints before God day and night; he is called an adversary, and a roaring lion, because he goeth about seeking whom he may devour; he is called the destroyer, because he maketh it his constant study how to destroy men, (both body and soul forever,) by his temptations and devices, &c. Oh! what maliciousness Satan sheweth against the gospel of Jesus Christ, in raising such opposition against it in the hearts of men; and what enmity he evidences against the souls of men, by keeping them in a constant commotion and perplexity of mind, and in defeating all the arguments and reasonings of the soul on the nature, excellency, necessity, and advantage of true religion. Thus Satan answers to his names and characters, and faithfully keeps up his titles, and prides himself in being the God of this world, the spirit that works in the children of disobedience, a ruler of darkness, and prince of the power of the air; whom let the saints resist.

The fifth Remedy is, seriously to consider, that it is safe for the soul to resist Satan peremptorily, but dangerous to dispute.

ZECHARIAH iii. 1, 2.
The Lord rebuke thee, O Satan.

To make present and peremptory resistance against Satan's temptations, yea, to bid defiance to them at

the first sight, in the name of the Lord, is your safety ; but to begin, with old mother Eve, to enter a
contest, by argumentation and vain disputings, would
prove your ruin and sad defeat. Mrs. Catharine
Eretterge, once after a great conflict with Satan,
said, " Reason not with me, I am but a weak woman;
if thou hast any thing to say, say it to my Christ, he
is my advocate, my strength, and my redeemer, and
he shall plead my cause." Men must not think to
resist Satan's craft with their craftiness ; he shoots
with Satan in his own bow, who thinks by vain dis-
puting and reasoning to vanquish him. It is your
greatest wisdom and highest honor peremptorily to
withstand the beginnings of a temptation ; for second thoughts and after remedies generally come too
late. Then let the saints peremptorily resist Satan
at his first appearance to insnare the soul : and when
Satan standeth at your right hand, like Joshua, say,
" The Lord rebuke thee, O Satan."

The sixth Remedy is, solemnly to consider, that
Satan suits his temptations to the constitutions and
inclinations of the saints.

LUKE xxii. 31.

*Satan hath desired to have you, that he may sift you
as wheat.*

Satan is a restless, subtle, and unwearied enemy,
who carefully studies both the constitution and in-

clination of the object he intends to devour; therefore he pries into the various powers and faculties of
the soul to find out the most likely member to accept his device, and if he finds your knowledge to
be weak and unstable, he will tempt you to error ;
if your conscience be tender, he will tempt you to
scrupulosity, and too much preciseness ; if your
conscience be liberal and large, he will tempt you to
carnal confidence and security; if you are bold spir-
ited, he will tempt you to presumption; if you are
timorous, he will tempt you to desperation ; if flexi-
ble, to inconstancy ; if proud, to stiffness and gross
folly, &c.; therefore, when you have obtained one
victory, do not cast aside your bow, but be ready to
meet a second and a third : and, certainly, he only
who makes a strong and constant resistance can gain
the conquest, and put his enemy to flight, and be de-
clared conqueror.   Still let us remember, that it is
but for a season that Satan departs from us, that he
may return with more force.

CHAP. XXIV.

SATAN HATH HIS DEVICES TO DESTROY AND INSNARE
THE GREAT AND HONORABLE IN THE WORLD. HIS
FIRST DEVICE IS BY WORKING THEM UP TO SEEK
THEMSELVES IN THEIR GREATNESS.

ESTHER vi. 6.

*Haman thought in his heart, To whom would the
king delight to do honor, &c, but to myself.*

Now, saith Satan, the Lord has given you both
riches and honor; you ought therefore, to study
how you can best establish yourselves, and your
children after you, in the high and honorable circle
of life Providence has placed you in : and the only
way to keep up your greatness and honorableness
amongst men, is by a diligent attention to your own
selves : seek your own glory and greatness; try
to advantage yourselves by raising, enriching, and
securing yourselves in those high and honorable
titles and places in the world. Oh ! saith Satan,
it does not become a nobleman, a statesman, nor
a monarch, to trouble themselves with religion, or
to make themselves so little in the world as to be
found amongst the poor, despised worshippers of
God. See Pharaoh, Ahab, Rehoboam, Jeroboam,
Absalom, Joab, Haman, &c. But were the scrip-

tures silent, our own observation and experience do abundantly evidence the way and the method of Satan to destroy the great and honorable, to bury their names in the dust and their souls in hell, by drawing them wholly to mind themselves in all things, to love themselves, to seek themselves, and to enlarge, enrich and ennoble themselves, that they may be great and honorable in the earth.

The precious Remedies against this device of Satan are these :

First. Solemnly to consider that self-love and self-seeking is attended with a train of evils and sins.

2 TIMOTHY iii. 2.
For men shall be lovers of their own selves.

Self-seeking is a sin that puts men upon a world of other sins ; upon sins not only against the law of God and the doctrines of the gospel, but that are against the very laws of nature. It was this that put the Pharisees upon opposing Christ, Judas upon betraying, and Pilate upon condemning Christ; this put Gehazi upon lying, Balaam upon cursing, and Saul and Absalom upon plotting David's ruin. What but self-seeking put Pharaoh and Haman upon contriving to destroy the Jews?

Self-glory and honor put men upon the ways and means of oppression and violence, that they would sell the righteous for silver, and the poor for a pair of shoes, &c.; it constrains men to use wicked balances, and the bag of deceitful weights. Self-seeking is like a deluge, that threatens to overthrow the world; and the love of self is the root of all hatred of others; first lovers of their own selves, then covetous, boasters, proud, blasphemers, &c., and then fierce, despisers of those that are good, and so become finally lovers of pleasures more than lovers of God, having a form of godliness, but denying the power thereof: from such turn away.

The second Remedy is, carefully to consider, that self-seeking doth exceedingly abase a man.

Ezekiel xxi. 25, 26, 27.
Exalt him that is low and abase him that is high.

So much of self doth strip the great and honorable of all their royalty and glory, and render them low and unworthy in the esteem of wise and prudent men. Of a lord, an esquire, &c. it makes a man become a servant to the creature, yea, a slave to slaves, as you may see in the word of God of various persons and characters, who have destroyed themselves through too much self-seeking. It is this that transforms a man into all shapes and forms, now as an angel of light, anon as an angel of darkness; at this moment deciding for God and for true religion, in the next plainly and openly opposing both; at one time supporting the cause of the poor and needy, and at another distressing and casting of them down to the ground. Self-seekers, whether among the great and honorable, or among the middle and lower class of men, are the basest of persons; for there is nothing so base, so low, and so poor, but what they will bow down to, in order to indulge self. Oh! that the great and honorable may not abase themselves, to their utter ruin, by seeking self in all that they do.

The third Remedy is, seriously to consider, that the God of glory hath denounced heavy woes upon self-seekers.

MICAH ii. 1, 2.
Wo to them that devise iniquity, &c.

Seriously consider that God hath poured out dreadful curses and woes, in that holy book called the Bible, upon all self-seekers, whether high or low, rich or poor, noble or ignoble. As woe to them that join house to house, that lay field to field, till there be no place, that they may be placed alone in the midst of the earth: so woe to him that increaseth that which is not his, and to him that ladeth himself with thick clay. Habakkuk ii. 6, 9, 10, 11, 12. Woe to him that coveteth an evil cov-

eteousness to his house, that he may set his nest on
high, &c. Woe to him that buildeth a town with
blood, and that establisheth a city by iniquity. The
materials of a house built by oppression, shall come
as joint-witnesses; the stones of the wall shall cry,
Lord, we were built by blood and violence; and
the beams shall answer, True, Lord, even so it is.
And woe unto them that decree unrighteous decrees,
&c., that turn aside the needy from judgment, and
take away the right from the poor, &c. Isaiah xv.
1, 2. By these scriptures you see that self-seekers
labor like a woman in travail, but their birth proves
their death.

The fourth Remedy is, attentively to consider the
noble example of those worthy saints and great men,
recorded in the scriptures, who all lived a life of
self-denial.

NEHEMIAH v. 14, 15.

*Yea, even their servants bear rule over the people;
but so have not I, because of the fear of God.*

What bright and illustrious examples of saints
and nobles, that have denied themselves, and prefer-
red the public good before their own particular advantage, may be found among both human and divine records, that are worthy of your imitation!
Moses was a man of a noble spirit, though a great
man and a ruler: the Lord said unto him, " I will

destroy this people, and blot out their name from under heaven; and I will make of thee a nation mightier and greater than they." Oh! but this offer would not take with Moses; for he began to pray for the people of Israel, and refused to give the Lord any rest until he had pardoned them. Ah! should God make such an offer to many who are called great, &c. in our time, what would become of the poor and the needy? Augustus Cæsar loved his people and commonwealth so highly, that he called it his own daughter, and refused to be called lord over his country, only styling himself a father of his people. But above all, let me not forget to give you the example of Jesus Christ, the only begotten Son of God, who emptied himself and became poor, that he might enrich, save and glorify poor sinners. Oh! that our great and honorable men would remember Jesus Christ.

The fifth Remedy is, solemnly to consider, that self-seeking is a great let and hindrance to the soul in divine objects.

JEREMIAH xlv. 5.
Seekest thou great things for thyself? Seek them not.

This solemn truth you might learn from the conduct of the prophets, and apostles of Jesus Christ, who, when they were favored with some unusual discovery and vision from God, were generally carried out of themselves, even to the loss of their own peace, &c. Self blinds the soul, that it cannot see the beauty of Christ, nor any excellency in holiness; it distempers the palate, that a man cannot taste sweetness in the word of God, nor in the ways of God, nor in the society of the people of God; it shuts the hand against the unsearchable riches of Christ, and hardens the heart against all the kind and gracious entreaties of Christ. Self makes the soul an empty vine and a barren wilderness. There cannot be a greater hindrance to the soul in all the duties of piety than self-seeking.—Oh! this is that enemy that keeps many precious souls from looking after God and the glorious things of eternity; and that causeth them to neglect and disregard the things that make for their peace. Oh! that you would first seek the kingdom of God, and his righteousness, that all other things might be added unto you in covenant love.

The sixth Remedy is, seriously to consider, that self-seekers are self losers and self-destroyers.

17*

OBADIAH 3, 4.

The pride of thine heart hath deceived thee, &c.
I will bring thee down saith the Lord.

Absalom and Judas seek themselves, and hang themselves; Saul seeks himself, and kills himself; Ahab s eks himself, and loses himself, his crown, and kingdom; Pharaoh seeks himself, and over-throws himself and his mighty army in the Red Sea; Cain sought himself, and slew two at once, his brother and his own soul; Haman sought him-self, and lost himself; the princes and presidents sought themselves and the ruin of Daniel, but ru-ined themselves, their wives and children. That which self-seekers think should be a staff to support them, becomes (by the hand of justice) an iron rod to break them; that which they would have as springs to refresh them, becomes a gulf, utterly to consume them. The crosses of self-seekers shall always exceed their mercies; their pain, their pleas-ure; and their torments, their comforts. Every self-seeker is a self-tormentor, a self-destroyer; he carries a hell, an executioner in his own bosom. Oh! that all, both great and small, that seek them-selves, may remember these things, and depart from that dangerous thing self, and may find pardon and eternal life through Jesus Christ our Lord. Amen.

CHAP. XXV.

THE SECOND DEVICE OF SATAN TO INSNARE AND DE-
STROY THE WISE, THE GREAT, AND THE HONORA-
BLE IN THE WORLD, IS BY ENGAGING THEM AGAINST
THE PEOPLE OF THE MOST HIGH.

ACTS xxvi. 11.
Being exceedingly mad against them.

Now, saith Satan, the learned and the wise in the
world are not to be brought upon the same low and
illiterate condition with the vulgar and unlearned;
your parts and faculties are more noble and refined,
and must be therefore capable to understand all
things needful in matters of religion, and have a just
right to enforce your doctrines with all the authority
and powers vested in you, (as the wisdom of the wise
is found in you,) only to interpret scripture doctrine,
and to declare others, who may oppose you, to be
erroneous and schismatics. To the great and honorable, Satan saith, You see those foolish and ignorant people that will not obey the authority of the
learned, but will still go on professing things that are
too high for them to comprehend, and things which
neither our forefathers nor we can understand; let us
consider what steps we should take to put a stop to the
spreading of these errors: we will use that power and
authority which our titles and estates have put into our

hands, to influence them to obey us ; or we must have recourse to that weight of legal authority which our office gives unto us, to restrain them. Thus Satan puts the great and honorable upon the saints.

———

The precious Remedies against this device of Satan are these :

First. Carefully to consider, that the sons of God are great and noble in grace and holiness, while the children of this world are only great and noble in gifts and gold.

LAMENTATIONS iv. 2.
The precious sons of Zion, comparable to fine gold.

The learned and the great may transcend the saints in parts and in gold, but the far greater part of them, when compared to the sons of God, are both poor and deficient in grace and holiness. There may be, and often we see it is so, among men of gifts, great abilities and attainments, though there is little or no grace of God in them ; and where we find but small parts and abilities in the saints, there shall we find great grace and holiness. You may be higher than others in gifts of knowledge, utterance, learning, &c., and those very souls that you despise are higher in their communion with God, in their delighting in God, in their dependance upon God, in their affections to God, and in their humble, holy, and unblameable walking before God. It is folly and madness in a man to make light of and slight another, because he is not so wise, so rich, or so honorable in titles or in yellow dust as he, when he is a thousand thousand times greater and richer in jewels and pearls than he. The spirit of the Lord will not always suffer his choicest jewels of grace and holiness to be buried under the straw and stubble of gifts and abilities. Let me therefore entreat the wise, the great, and the honorable of the earth, to consider, that grace and holiness are the best riches.

The second Remedy is, seriously to consider, that your gifts wither away, your finest parts are blasted, and your titles perish forever in the dust; but the saints endure, and reign in grace and holiness for ever and ever.

PROVERBS x. 25.
The wicked is no more ; but the righteous is an everlasting foundation.

Saints are God's jewels. How rare, precious, comely, excellent, and useful! With what care and exactness are they sought out by the Lord! How highly are they polished by himself; and how brightly must they shine before him for ever in his glory! Saints are comparable to fine gold : how the furnace of affliction purges away their dross, and refines them as gold and silver are refined! And how highly the Lord esteems them, as his portion and wealth! Yea, the saints are the apple of God's eye: how dear to him, how carefully defended and preserved by him! How deeply he sympathizes with them! And how highly is he, provoked with, and incensed against them that injure them? for they touch the apple of his eye. There is no readier way for men, in all their greatness and glory, to wither away and die, than to pride themselves in their gifts and abilities, and employ them against the saints, against the men whom God loves, and whom Jesus Christ has set his heart upon. Oh! that the wise, the great, and honorable in the land, would think upon these jewels and rich pearls in Christ's crown; and seek, above all things, to be found in him.

The third Remedy is, solemnly to consider, that none have engaged against the saints, but have been ruined by the God of saints.

Zechariah ii. 8.

He that toucheth you, toucheth the apple of his eye.

Divine justice hath been too hard for all that have opposed the saints : he hath reproved kings for their sakes, saying, " Touch not mine anointed, nor do my prophets no harm." When men of Pharoah's,

Balaam's and Haman's spirits and principles have been engaged against the saints, how hath the angel of the Lord met them in the way, and jostled their bones against the wall! How hath he broken their backs and necks, and by his sword cut them off in the prime of their days and in the height of their sins! Ah! how hath divine justice poured out their blood as water upon the ground! How hath he laid their honor and glory in the dust, who, in the pride and madness of their hearts said, as Pharoah, " We will pursue, we will overtake, we will divide the spoils; our lusts shall be satisfied upon them," &c. But in the things wherein they have spoken proudly, justice hath been above them: history abounds in nothing more than in instances of this kind. Oh! my friends, what a harvest hath hell had in the days that are past of those who have engaged against the Lamb, and those that are called chosen and faithful! Oh! that you may never forget these things.

The fourth Remedy is, attentively to consider, that you are much obligated and indebted to the saints for all the mercies you enjoy.

GENESIS xviii. 26.
I will spare all the place for their sakes.

Were it not for the saints' sake, God would quickly make the heavens to be as brass, and the earth as iron: they are the props that bear up the world from falling about thy ears, and that keep the iron rod from breaking thy bones to pieces. Ah! had not the saints many times cast themselves into the breach betwixt God's wrath and you, you had surely been cut off from the land of the living. Many a nation, many a city, many a family, and many an individual is surrounded with blessings, and has escaped severe judgments, for Joseph's sakes that live among them : had it not been for their sakes, God would have stript thee of thy robes and glory, and have set thee upon the dunghill. Mary, queen of Scots, said, "I am more afraid of the prayers of John Knox than an army of ten thousand men." "When the danger is over the saint is forgotten," is a French proverb. The emperor Marcus Antonius, being in great distress, with his whole army, and likely to perish for want of water, one of his lieutenants told him, that he had heard that the christians could obtain any thing of God, by their prayers; he called for all the christians in his army, and desired them to pray; they readily obeyed, and the Lord sent deliverance.

The fifth Remedy is, seriously to consider, that you cannot engage against the saints, but you must also engage against God himself.

ACTS v. 38, 39.

Let them alone ; lest ye be found even to fight against
God.

Seriously consider, that to fight against a saint is
to fight against God himself; and who ever engaged
against God and prospered ?   Or who ever took up
the sword against him, but perished by the sword ?
God can confound you in a moment, and by the
word of his mouth can send you to hell, (at his sovereign will and pleasure,) before you can put into ex-
ecution any one of your wicked counsels against the
saints ; yea, and even turn your very counsels into
foolishness, and cause it to fall upon your own heads.
See, then, that you cannot fight against the saints,
but you must engage with God himself.   And what
greater madness can you display, than for weakness
itself to fight against almighty strength ?   There is
a near and gracious union between God and his
saints, more sacred and noble than all the unions upon earth : this union is so near, that you cannot
strike a believer but you must smite the Lord ; therefore he called out to one, saying, " Saul, Saul, why
persecutest thou me ?   It is hard for thee to kick
against the pricks."   Oh ! be it your greatest concern to lay down your weapons at his feet, and to
kiss the son of God.

The sixth Remedy is, solemnly to consider, that the wise, the great, and the honorable stand in the same need of Jesus Christ, as the poor and needy ; and there is every thing in him to encourage the rich, (as well as the poor,) believing in him.

ROMANS x. 11, 12.

The same Lord is rich unto all that call upon him.

Though it be said, not many wise men after the flesh, not many mighty, not many noble are called ; yet, blessed be God, it does not say, not any wise, not any mighty, or not any noble after the flesh are called. There are sufficient evidences in the scripture of some wise, some mighty, and some noble persons and kings, who have believed on Jesus Christ to the saving of their souls: and thank God he has not left himself without witnesses among the great in these days. If you look upon the names, titles, offices, nature and disposition of Jesus Christ, you will find nothing to discourage the great or the noble to look unto him and be saved. Christ is the soul's greatest good, the choicest good, the chiefest good, and the most necessary good to all sensible sinners, whether among the rich or the poor. Are you poor ? Christ hath gold to enrich you. Are you naked ? Christ hath white raiment to clothe you. Are you blind ? Christ hath eye-salve to enlighten you. Are you hungry ? Christ will be the true manna to feed you. Are you thirsty? He will be a well of living water to refresh you. Are you sick? He is a physician to cure you. And are you wounded, or a prisoner? He has healing under his wings, and he can command your prison doors to be opened.

CHAP. XXVI.

SATAN HATH HIS DEVICES TO DESTROY THE SONS OF
GOD. AND HIS FIRST DEVICE IS BY WORKING THEM
UP TO BE STRANGE, JEALOUS, AND THEN TO DIVIDE
FROM ONE ANOTHER.

GALATIANS v. 15.

*But if ye bite aud devour one another, take heed
that ye be not consumed.*

SATAN'S main glory over the Christian and professing world, is in the separations and divisions
which he encourages in the pride of the human heart,
by creating a shyness with one another, and then
working them up to be strange and dissatisfied with
each other, until jealousy creeps in amongst them,
and then nothing can do but a rent; a division takes
place, and Satan cherishes the flame; the pride of
the heart carries forward the contest, and justifies
each party to be in the right; they divide, they begin to bite and devour one another. Now professing people become the worst of enemies to one
another, and will both preach and work against one
another, as if they were each party contending for
different kingdoms and inheritances. Satan thus
comes off victorious over religion. See, saith he,

to the world, what a people those professing saints
are ! Who more envious, hateful, and contentious
than they? Their religion cannot be right, because they cannot keep together ; but divide into so
many parties, doctrines, and modes of worship.

The precious Remedies against this device of Satan are these :

First. Carefully to consider, that love and unity
make most for your own safety and security.

EPHESIANS iv 3.
Endeavoring to keep the unity of the spirit, &c.

If the professing friends of the gospel of Jesus
Christ were but of one heart and mind, where is the
power or enemy that could harm them? The world
may frown upon you, and Satan and men may plot
against your peace, but they cannot prevail. Unity
is the best bond of safety in every church and commonwealth : we shall be insuperable if we be inseparable. There was a temple of Concord amongst
the heathens, &c.; should it not be so amongst Christians, who are, or who ought to be, the temples of
the Holy Ghost? How lively is this doctrine repre-
sented in the conduct of a certain king, that gave
his last and dying advice to eighty sons, by com-

manding a bundle of arrows, fast bound together, to be given to them to break? They all tried, but they could not break one of the arrows, because they were so fast bound together: the king then ordered the band to be cut, and his sons to try again; they did so, and readily broke them all. Then the royal father applied it thus: " My sons, so long as you keep together you will be invincible; but if the band of union be broke, you will be broken in pieces." So long as the sons of God keep together they conquer.

The second Remedy is, seriously to dwell more upon one another's graces, than upon one another's weaknesses.

PHILLIPIANS ii. 1, 2, 3, 4.
Look not every man on his own things, but, &c.

It is a sad thing that saints should have many eyes to behold one another's infirmities, and not one eye to see each other's graces. Vespasian was more ready to conceal the vices of his friends than their virtues. Can we seriously think of this condnct of an heathen, and not blush? Tell me, ye saints, is it not a more sweet, comfortable, and delightful thing to look more upon one another's graces, than upon one another's weaknesses? What pleasure, what delight, or what comfort can there be in looking upon the enemies, the wounds, the sores, the sicknesses, the

diseases, and the nakedness of your friends? Sin
and infirmities are the soul's enemies, the soul's
wounds, and the soul's sicknesses, &c. &c. Ah!
what a heart hath that man or woman got, that loves
to dwell upon those things that cause both pain
and shame in every sincere Christian! Doth not
God himself look more upon the graces of his people than upon their weaknesses? Yea, God puts his
fingers upon the scars of his people, that no blemish
may be found upon them. Let us resemble our
heavenly Father.

The third Remedy is, solemnly to consider the
things wherein the saints are agreed and satisfied
with each other.

EPHESIANS v. 1, 2.

Followers of God, as dear children, &c.

Oh! that you could but dwell more upon those
choice and excellent things wherein the saints are at
peace and in union with one another, rather than
upon those things wherein they differ, how soon
should we see sinful hearts and tempers changed, and
love, fellowship, and concord in sweet abundance
flow to every pious soul! The saints are agreed in
most interesting and essential truths, and differ,
comparatively, in a few things: they agree in the
greatest and weightiest matters concerning God, Jesus Christ, the Holy Spirit, the scriptures, &c. Oh!

what a sad thing it was for a heathen (reproving
Christians) to reproach Christianity with saying,
" Beasts are not so cruel and mischievous to men, as
the Christians are to one another." Shall Herod
and Pilate agree? Shall Turks and Pagans agree?
Shall bears and lions, tigers and wolves, yea, shall a
legion of devils agree in one body; and shall not
saints agree, who differ only in such things as have
least of the heart of God in them, and that shall never keep them from meeting in heaven?

The fourth Remedy is, carefully to consider, that
it is your duty to judge your own selves.

1 CORINTHIANS xi. 31.

For if we would judge ourselves, we should not be
judged.

Were Christians more taken up in judging themselves, and condemning their own selves, they would
not be so apt to judge and censure others, and to
carry themselves so bitterly and evilly towards those
that differ from them. There are no souls in the
world that are so careful and fearful to judge others, as those who do most faithfully judge themselves;
nor prudent in making a righteous judgment of men
and things, as those who cautiously judge their own
hearts: there are none that make such sweet con-
structions and charitable interpretations of men and
things, as those that are diligent in finding out their

own hearts ; there are none in the world that tremble to think evil, to speak evil, or to do evil to others, as those that acquaint themselves with their own
evils.   One request I have to make to you that live
much in judging others, and are too great strangers
in judging yourselves ; to you that are so prone to
judge and condemn rashly, falsely, and unrighteously;
and that is, that you will every morning dwell a little time, attentively upon these scriptures : Matthew
vii. 1, 2.   John vii. 24.   " Judge not according to
the appearance," &c.   Romans xiv. 3, 4.   " Who
art thou that judgest another man's servant?" &c.

The fifth Remedy is, attentively to consider, that
the miseries of discord and strife amongst the followers of Christ, are great and ruinous to the interest
of true religion.

JAMES iii. 14, 16.
*For where envying and strife is, there is confusion
and every evil work.*

Ah ! how doth the name of Christ and the truth
of Christ, bleed and suffer by the discord of professing people !   How are many souls, that are en-
tering into the ways of God, hindered and sadly
cast back again into the world, and the mouths of
the wicked opened, and their hearts hardened
against God, and the gospel of Jesus Christ despised, preachers and preaching set at nought, and

esteemed foolishness! &c. How are the saints of
God distressed, and weak minds turned out of the
right way, whilst enemies are strengthened and daily increased, and the wicked rejoice to see discord
and strife abound among the followers of the Lamb!
Remember that the disagreement of the saints is
the devil's triumph. Dissolution is the daughter
of dissention. It was a notable saying of one,
" Take away strife, and call back peace, lest thou
lose a man thy friend, and the devil, an enemy, rejoice over you both." Who can sufficiently admire
the spirit and conduct of Abraham towards Lot?
Genesis xiii. 8. Let there be no bitterness nor dis-
sension between us for we are brethren. So let the
saints consider one another as fellow members of
the same body, as fellow soldiers under the same
captain, as fellow sufferers under the same enemies,
and as fellow travelers and citizens, and fellow heirs
of the same crown &c.

The sixth Remedy is, solemnly to consider, that
it is no disparagement to a saint to be first in seeking
peace and union, but rather an honor.

ROMANS xiv. 19.

Let us follow after the things that make for peace,
&c.

Was not Abraham the elder, and a far more great
and worthy man than Lot, both in temporals and spir-

ituals? And yet he first seeks peace and union with his inferior; and the spirit of God has recorded it as an honor to Abraham. And shall I not be justified in saying, that the great and glorious God is, first in seeking and bringing about a peace between himself and guilty sinners? Ah! souls, it is not a base and low thing, but a godlike thing, though we are wronged by others, to be the first in seeking after peace. There is a remarkable story of Aristippus, a heathen, who went of his own accord to Æschines, his enemy, and said, "Shall we never be reconciled till we become a table talk to all the country?" Æschines answered, that he would most gladly be at peace with him. "Remember, then," said Aristippus, "that although I am the elder and better man, yet I sought first unto thee." "Thou art, indeed," replied Æschines, "a far better man than I; for I began the qurrael, but thou the reconcilement." Oh! let it be your prayer, and mine also, that this heathen may not rise in judgment against the flourishing professors of these days. Psalm lxiv. 3. "Who whet their tongues like a sword," &c.

CHAP. XXVII.

THE SECOND DEVICE OF SATAN AND THE HUMAN HEART TO DESTROY THE PEACE OF THE SAINTS, IS BY REPRESENTING TO THEM THE GREATNESS AND VILENESS OF SIN, TO KEEP THE SOUL FROM RESTING ON CHRIST.

JEREMIAH iii. 5.

Thou hast spoken and done evil things as thou couldst.

WHAT, saith Satan, dost thou think that thou shalt ever obtain mercy by Christ, that hast sinned with so high a hand against Christ? Hast not thou slighted the tenders of his grace? Hast not thou grieved the spirit of his grace? Hast not thou despised the word of his grace? And hast thou not trampled under thy feet the blood of his covenant, by which alone thou mightest have been saved, pardoned, purged, and accepted of God? In short thou hast both spoken and done all the evil that thou couldest against Jesus Christ, against the followers of Jesus Christ, and against the gospel of Jesus Christ. No, no, saith Satan and thine heart, he hath mercy for others, but not for thee; pardon for others, but not for thee; righteousness for others, but not for thee; therefore it is

all in vain for thee to think of believing in
Christ, receiving, and embracing of Christ, and
of resting or relying upon Christ for everlasting
salvation and blessedness, according to the gospel,
all which they enjoy who cast and lean the whole
weight of their guilty souls upon him, as their
Lord and Saviour; but as for thee, there is no hope
that Christ can receive thee into his arms.

———

The precious Remedies against this device of
Satan and the human heart are these :

First. Carefully to consider, that the greater
your sins are, the more you stand in need of Jesus
Christ.

Isaiah xliii. 25.

*I, even I am he that blotteth out thy transgressions,
for mine own sake, &c.*

Surely the greater your burden is, the more you
stand in need of one to bear it; the deeper the
wound is, the more need there is of the surgeon;
the more dangerous the disease is, the more need
there is of the physician. Who but a madman
would argue thus? " My burden is great, therefore I will not call out for help; my wound is deep,
therefore I will not seek out for a balm; my disease is
dangerous, therefore I will not go to the physician."

19

'Tis spiritual madness, 'tis the devil's logic to argue thus: " My sins are great, therefore I will not go to Christ; I dare not rest, lean and believe on Christ for salvation," &c. Now the Spirit of God directs the soul to a contrary reasoning on this subject, thus: "The greater my sins are, the more I stand in need of Jesus Christ to be my Saviour; I need his mercy to pardon, his grace to keep, his spirit to sanctify, his blood to wash and cleanse me from all my sins; and I stand in need of his power to support my soul in coming to him: I will therefore arise and go to Christ alone for help, in this my time of need; for who but Christ can pardon great sins? And who like him that delights to pardon, and who is both able and willing?"

The second Remedy is, seriously to consider, that the greatest sinners have obtained mercy in coming to Jesus Christ.

1 TIMOTHY i. 15.
*Jesus Christ came into the world to save **sinners**, of whom I am chief.*

Manassah was a notorious sinner; he erected altars for Baal, he worshipped and served all the hosts of heaven, he caused his sons to pass through the fire, he gave himself up to wickedness, and caused the streets of Jerusalem to run down with innocent blood; yet after all this, by the grace of God, his

heart is humbled, and he seeks unto God for mercy
and forgiveness; and the Lord was entreated of
him, heard and accepted his supplication and crowned him with loving kindness and tender mercy.
2 Chronicles xxxiii. 12, 13.   Mary Magdalen was
a great offender, and out of her Christ cast seven
devils; yet she obtained mercy and pardon through
Jesus' blood.   Saul, of Tarsus, was a blasphemer,
a persecutor, and an injurious man; yet he also obtained mercy.   What though thou art a rebellious
child, a vile sinner, and an unworthy creature, yet
remember that Jesus, after his resurrection, appeared
first to Mary and Peter, two of the greatest of sinners,
and the most unworthy, in order to comfort and
strengthen the worst of sinners coming unto God
by him; Christ has ascended up on high and received
gifts for thee, even for the rebellious.

The third Remedy is carefully to consider, that
Jesus Christ has no where exempted the greatest
sinner from coming to him for rest and salvation.

JOHN vi. 37.

And him that cometh to me I will in no wise cast
out.

Well, saith Jesus Christ, if any man will come
to me, let him be more or less sinful, more or less
worthy; let him be never so guilty, never so filthy,
never so rebellious, and never so leprous, &c., yet

if he is a comer to me, I will never cast him off.
Now, sinner, art thou made a willing soul, in the
day of his power, this should be thy encouragement; that he that has given thee desire to seek
rest and pardon in Jesus, is the very same that saith,
I will not cast thee off. Christ was born in an inn,
to show that he recieveth all that come; his garments were divided into four parts, to shew that
comers out of all parts of the earth shall find mercy
with him. Jesus Christ is an all-sufficient Saviour,
therefore he can save the greatest as well as the
least of sinners. Ah! coming souls, tell Jesus.
Christ, that he hath not excluded you from mercy,
&c., therefore you are resolved that you will sit,
wait, weep, and knock at mercy's door, till he shall
say, " Soul, be of good cheer, your sins are forgiven," &c.

The fourth Remedy is, solemnly to consider, that
the greatness of our sins (as coming souls to Jesus
Christ) doth magnify the riches and freeness of the
love of Christ to the vilest of the vile.

1 TIMOTHY i. 16.

*All long-suffering, for a pattern to them which
should hereafter believe on him to life everlasting.*

Yea, might I not say to the coming sinner, that
the greater sinner thou seest thyself to be, the dearer thou wilt be to Christ, when he shall behold the

as the travail of his soul. Christ hath paid most, prayed most, sighed most, wept most, and bled most for thee; therefore thou art dearer to him in his heart; as Jacob esteemed Rachel dearer to him than Leah. The dearer we pay for any thing, the more we love and long after that thing. Ah! coming, sensible sinner, thou that wouldst gladly lay hold of Jesus as thy Lord, but Satan keeps thee back, through thy sins, learn that the greater thy sins, the more rich and free must the grace and love of Christ be in thy acceptance and pardon; this maketh heaven and earth to ring with his praise, that he loves those that are most unlovely, that he shows most favor to them that have sinned most highly against him, and that he can most freely pardon and justify the ungodly, that believe and rest on him.

The fifth Remedy is, attentively to consider, that the longer you believe Satan, and keep off from embracing Christ, the stronger your sins will grow.

1 JOHN v. 4.
This is the victory that overcometh the world, even our faith.

While you keep off from Christ, you will deprive yourselves of that strength and power which alone is able to make you trample down strength, lead captivity captive, and slay the great Goliahs, that

19*

bid defiance to Christ. 'Tis faith in Christ only that binds the strong man, that stops the issue of blood, and that makes a man strong in resisting and happy in conquering. Sin, great or small, always dies most where faith lives most; the most believing soul, is the most sin-mortifying soul. Ah! sinner, remember this; that there is no way on earth effectually to be rid of the guilt, filth, and power of sin, but by coming to and believing on Jesus Christ. It is not a soul-resolving, it is not a complaining, it is not a mourning over sin and Satan, but a soul-believing, that will make thee divinely victorious over that body of sin, which to this day, has been too strong for thee: *behold*, therefore, *the Lamb of God*.

The sixth Remedy is, seriously to consider, that the promise of grace and mercy is made to returning or coming souls.

HEBREWS vii. 25.

Wherefore he is able also to save them to the uttermost that come unto God by him.

Oh! What exceeding great and precious promises hath God made known to coming sinners in the gospel? And, therefore, though thou art the greatest of sinners, and ever so vile in thine own eyes, yet if thou art a comer, a returner unto God through Jesus Christ, thou shalt find mercy; yea, God shall

be thy God, Christ shall be thy Christ, the Spirit
shall be thy Spirit, to sanctify and comfort thee;
pardon shall be thine, justification shall be thine,
eternal life shall be thine; yea all things in heaven
and in earth shall be thine, and thou art Christ's
for ever and for ever.   Ah! soul, it is not thy great
sins and transgressions that exclude thee from mercy, but thy unbelief, in not coming to Jesus Christ.
Jesus' heart, Jesus' arms are opened wide to accept every coming soul.   It is, therefore, not simply
the greatness of thy sin and unworthiness, but thy
peremptorily persisting in sin, and rejecting Jesus
Christ, that will be thy eternal overthrow, if thou
art cast off.

CHAP. XXVIII.

THE THIRD DEVICE OF SATAN TO KEEP POOR SIN-
NERS FROM BELIEVING AND RESTING ON JESUS
CHRIST, IS BY REPRESENTING TO THEM THEIR
GREAT UNWORTHINESS, AND WANT OF NECESSARY
QUALIFICATIONS.

LUKE iii. 8.

Bring forth fruits worthy of repentance.

AH! saith Satan, as thou art worthy of the greatest misery, so thou art unworthy of the least crum
of mercy. What! dost thou think that ever Christ
will own, receive, and embrace such an unworthy
wretch as thou art? No, no: if there was any good
thing in thee, then Christ might be inclined to entertain thee for a while at least; but there is no worthiness in thee to attract Christ, even so much as into thine house: and how much more unworthy art
thou to entertain him in thy heart? Now, saith Satan if thou hadst but such and such qualifications
and preparations, then thou mighest expect the Lord
would accept thee. But thou art not thus and thus
humbled, sanctified, and made holy; thou art not
heart-sick of sin; thou hast not been under such
alarming terrors and grief as others have been: neither hast thou been so deeply ravished with a sense

of Jesus' love, and the joys of heaven, as such and such of God's children have been.

The precious Remedies against this device of Satan are these:

First. Carefully to consider, that if the soul must keep back from Christ until it be worthy, the soul will never close with Christ.

1 CORINTHIANS i. 30.
But of him are ye in Christ Jesus, who of God is made unto us wisdom, &c.

God hath laid up all worthiness and qualifications for souls, (coming to Christ,) in his only begotten Son; and, therefore, if the soul will keep off from Christ until it be worthy, it will never embrace Christ, nor ever be one with Christ; and there is no way which even infinite wisdom can find out to make the unworthy soul worthy, but by believing, accepting, and relying upon Christ. Believing in Christ, of slaves, will make you worthy sons; of enemies, it will make you worthy friends. God will count none qualified, nor call any holy, nor carry himself towards any as prepared and qualified for his presence, but such as believe in Christ, and who receive him of God, made unto them wisdom, righteousness,

sanctification, and redemption ; and who thus esteem themselves made worthy and qualified in and
through Christ's person, righteousness, satisfaction,
and intercession.   Lord, let me ever stand thus complete and worthy in thy sight through Jesus Christ,
my Lord and Saviour.

The second Remedy is, seriously to consider,
that God hath no where in all the scriptures required
any worthiness in the creature before coming to
Christ.'

JOHN vi. 40.

*That every one which seeth the Son, and believeth
on him, may have everlasting life.*

If you make a diligent search through all the
book of God, you shall not find (from the first line
in Genesis to the last in Revelations) one word that
speaks out God's requiring any worthiness in the soul
before believing in Jesus Christ : and why, then,
should that be made a bar and hindrance to thy faith,
which God doth no where require of thee before
thou comest to Christ, that thou mayest live ?   The
law requires a full and perfect obedience ; but thou
art seeking life and salvation in Christ, who has
magnified the law, and made it honorable.   Ah !
sinner, Satan objects thy unworthiness against thee,
not out of love to holiness, nor regard to Christ,
but only out of a design to keep Christ and thy soul.

asunder forever; and therefore let me advise thee, in the face of all thy unworthiness, to rest thy soul upon Christ: come to Christ, embrace Christ, yea, lean thy everlasting concerns upon Christ, knowing that none ever yet received Christ but unworthy souls, and souls who have all lamented their unworthiness and their sins, and yet cast themselves at Jesus' feet, saying, "Save, Lord, or I perish for ever."

The third Remedy is, attentively to consider, that it is the pride of thy heart that puts thee upon seeking worthiness to bring to Christ.

Isaiah lv. 1, 2.

Wherefore do you spend your money upon that which is not bread, &c.

Let the soul but search carefully the spring of this objection against closing with Christ, and you will find that the pride and folly of your own hearts are moving you to look for worthiness in yourselves, to bring to Christ. Oh! you would fain bring something to Christ that might render you acceptable to him, for you cannot think of coming empty handed; and so, filthy and unclean, could you but wash away the outward stain it would give some pleasure. Infinite wisdom and goodness calls upon you to come as you are, moneyless, helpless, and hopeless souls, &c., but sinners are proud and foolish, and because they have no money, no worthiness to bring, they will not come, although he sweetly invites them to come to him without money and without price, nor of fitness fondly dream; for all the fitness he requires, is for you to see and feel your need of him. Ah! sinners, remember, that it is not so much the sense of your unworthiness, as your pride, that keeps you back from embracing Jesus Christ. Oh! consider this, all ye that spend your money for that which is not bread, and your labor for that which satisfieth not; when Jesus calls you to come to him for the true bread of eternal life, that you may eat and live for ever.

The fourth Remedy is, solemnly to consider, that such as have not been so and so prepared and qualified as Satan suggests, have received Christ, and been accepted and saved by him.

Acts xvi. 30, 31.

What must I do to be saved? And they said be-
. *lieve on the Lord Jesus Christ, &c.*

Pray what preparations and qualifications were found in Matthew, Zaccheus, Paul, the jailor, and Lydia, before their conversion? God is a free agent, to work by law or gospel, by smiles or frowns; by representing heaven or hell unto the sinner's view. God thunders from Mount Sinai upon some souls, and conquers them by thunderings; God speaks to others in a still, small voice, and by that prevails with them. Ye that are brought to Christ by the law, do not ye judge and condemn them that are brought to Christ by the gospel; and ye that are brought to Christ by the gospel, do not ye despise those that are brought to Christ by the law. Some, therefore, are brought to Christ, and embrace him, by storms, fire, and tempests; others by more easy and gentle gales of the Spirit. Thus the divine Spirit is free and sovereign in his works of conversion, and as the wind, which blows when, where, and how it pleases, without waiting for any sort of qualification or preparation in men. Thrice happy are those souls that are brought to Christ, whether it be in a winter's night or on a summer's day. Let the coming soul, then remember, that such as were received by Christ in years past, such he still welcomes and accepts without qualifications, &c.

The fifth Remedy is, seriously to consider, that the best preparation and qualification that a soul can bring to God, is faith in Jesus Christ.

ROMANS xiv. 23.
For whatsoever is not of faith is sin.

Believing in Christ is the grand and great thing which God requires, and that which the scriptures press upon men in the most solemn manner: he that believeth shall be saved, and he that believeth not shall be damned. But this same faith that leads the

20

soul to rest on Christ, is the gift of God, and the sole operation of the spirit of God. For a poor sinner, when convinced of the evil of sin, the wrath of God, and the spirituality of the law, instead of bringing forth any good qualifications to God, runs from creature to creature, from duty to duty, and from one vain refuge to another; and if any satisfaction or rest could be found in the creature, or in the duty, (did not divine faith lead the burdened soul to eye Christ as every way qualified for the coming sinner,) the soul would not find rest in Christ. Look up to God, and wait on him for that jewel faith, which is worth more than life itself; for without faith you cannot please God, nor be accepted of him. Whatever you may bring to God, if you come without faith, you will be rejected.

The sixth Remedy is, diligently to consider, that all true godly sorrow and mourning for sin flows from faith in Christ.

ZECHARIAH xii. 10.

They shall look on him whom they have pierced, and they shall mourn.

All that trouble of soul for sin, all that shame and pain, and all that sorrow and mourning, which is acceptable and delightful to God, yea, and prevalent with God, flows from believing in Christ; as the stream doth from the fountain, as the branch doth from the root, and as the effect doth from the cause. All gospel sorrow and mourning flow from believing in Christ. They shall first look, and then mourn. Christ is the greatest good, the choicest good, the chiefest good, and the most necessary good to poor sinners. When, therefore, the soul, by faith, is enabled to look upon Christ, in all his perfections, as the friend of sinners, conscious of the sins and transgressions that attend both the heart and life, the soul mourns before God that depravity and course which has wounded and cruelly pierced the Lord of glory afresh, and opened all his wounds. Thus let the coming sinner learn to come just as he is, and not to wait for qualifications, &c.

CHAP. XXIX.

AS SATAN DESTROYS THE SOULS OF MEN THROUGH
VARIOUS DEVICES, SO HE ALSO DECEIVETH MANY
TO THEIR ETERNAL RUIN, BY FALSE TEACHERS.

2 CORINTHIANS xi. 13, 14, 15.
False apostles, deceitful workers, &c. &c.

SATAN'S main design with false teachers is to oppose the faithful ministers of Jesus Christ, by raising
ill reports and reproaches upon their persons,
names and abilities. Thus Korah, Dathan and
Abiram, charged Moses and Aaron, that they took
too much upon them, seeing all the congregation
was holy. You take too much state, too much power, too much honor, and too much holiness upon
you; for what are you more than others? So
Ahab's false prophets fell upon good Michaiah.—
Yea, Paul, that great apostle of the Gentiles, had
his ministry undervalued, and his reputation blasted
by false teachers. 2 Corinthians x. 10. And so did
they unto our blessed Lord Jesus, who taught as
never man taught; for he taught as one having authority, and not as a Scribe; yet the Scribes and
Pharisees labored night and day to blast his credit
with the people: and just so the devil leadeth false
teachers unto this day. Oh! the reproaches and,

the contempt cast upon all the faithful ministers of the gospel by false apostles.

The precious Remedies against Satan and his false teachers are these:

First. Seriously to consider, that false teachers cover and color their dangerous principles with fair speeches and plausible pretences.

ROMANS xvi. 18.
By good words and fair speeches deceive the hearts of the simple.

Impostors impose upon thousands with fair words and flattering pretences, with high notions and golden expressions. How many in these days are bewitched and deceived by the magnificent words, lofty strains, and stately terms of deceivers? viz: Illumination, revelation, deification, and fiery triplicity. As strumpets paint their faces and deck and perfume their beds, the better to allure and de-- ceive simple souls, so do these false teachers put a great deal of paint and garnish upon their mos dangerous principles and blasphemies, that they may the better deceive and delude poor ignorant souls; they know that sugared poison goes down sweetly; they wrap up their most pernicious oul-killing pills in gold; and they allure through

20*

plausible appearances and pretences. Thus the simple are snared and taken, and by good words and fair speeches their hearts are deceived and their feet turned out of the way of truth. So God gave them up to believe a lie, that both the deceiver and the deceived might perish forever, who believed not the truth.

The second Remedy is, carefully to consider, that false teachers are men-pleasers.

GALATIANS i. 10.

For if I yet please men, I should not be the servant of Christ.

False teachers preach more to please the ear than to profit and edify the soul; they handle holy things rather with wit and human elegancy, than with fear and reverence. Flattery ruined Ahab, Herod, Nero, and Alexander. Not bitter, but flattering words do all the mischief, said Valerian, the Roman emperor. Isaiah xxx. 10. "Which say to the seers, see not, and to the prophets, prophesy not unto us right things; speak unto us smooth things, prophesy deceits." Jeremiah v. 30, 31. "A wonderful and horrible thing is committed in the land; the prophets prophesy falsely, and the priests bear rule by their means, and my people love to have it so: and what will you do in the end thereof?" False teachers are soul-undoers; they kiss and kill,

and cry peace, peace, until the soul falls into everlasting flames; and thus they are the faithful labor-
ers of Satan, who work with might and main, as
his messengers and ambassadors, to deceive, delude,
and forever undo the precious souls of men. These
false teachers lick and suck the blood of souls, and
as dogs devour the souls of men. Philippians iii.
2. Beware of them.

The third Remedy is, solemnly to consider, that
false teachers easily pass over the great and weighty
things of both law and gospel, and dwell upon those
things which are of less moment to souls.

MATTHEW xxiii. 23, 24.

*Woe unto you, &c. ye have omitted the weightier
matters of the law, judgment, mercy and faith.*

How easily these false teachers can omit the great
and glorious things of the gospel, and with an ea-
gerness of soul contend for those that are of the
least moment and concern to the souls of men.—
Hear the word of God on these characters. 1 Timothy i. 5, 6, 7. " Now the end of the commandment is charity out of a pure heart, and of a good
conscience, and of faith unfeigned; from which
some having swerved, have turned aside unto vain
jangling, desiring to be teachers of the law, and understanding neither what they say nor what they af-
firm." " Woe unto you Scribes and Pharisees, hy-

pocrites, for ye pay tithe of mint, and annise, and cummin, and have omitted the weightier matters of the law, judgment, mercy and faith; these ought ye to have done, and not to leave the others undone." Thus we see them nice in the lesser things of the law, and negligent in the greater. If such false teachers are not hypocrites in the grain, I know none in all the world: surely the earth groans to bear them, and hell must be fitted for them.

The fourth Remedy is, attentively to consider, that false teachers strive more to win over men to their opinions than to Christ, and to better their hearts and lives.

MATTHEW xxiii. 15.
Ye compass sea and land to make one proselyte &c.

These false teachers busy themselves from day to day about the heads, but not about the hearts of the children of men: the heart-work is counted enthusiasm and folly, nothing short of madness, and a monstrous and ridiculous absurdity in religion, and what is only fit for poor, weak, ignorant minds. In the days of Adrian, the emperor, one Bencosby gathered a multitude of Jews together, and called himself Bencocuba, the son of a star, applying that promise to himself, Numbers xxiv. 17. But he proved Barchosaba, the son of a lie: and so will all false teachers; for all their flourishes will at last prove them sons of lies. They make merchandise of men after they have proselyted them to their opinion; then they eye their goods more than their good, their fleece more than their souls: for they make every proselyte two-fold more the child of hell than themselves. Crates threw his money into the sea, resolving to drown it lest it should drown him: but these false teachers care not whom they drown, so they may have their money.

The fifth Remedy is, carefully to consider, that false teachers are rejected, and given up by God to follow their own evil ways, that they may stumble and fall (by their own folly) into the pit.

EZEKIEL xiii. 9.

And mine hand shall be upon their prophets that see vanity and that divine lies, &c.

When wicked men withstand the gracious doctrines of the gospel, and despise the spirit of grace, and throw off the word of God, then the Lord, in just judgment, casts them off from his care, and leaves them a prey to their own hearts and Satan. He who thinks himself too good and too great to be ruled by the word of God, will be found too vile to be owned by the Lord; and being left of God, the word and rod of God hardens his heart; and thus his spirit and conscience are given up by the hand of justice to be deceived and ensnared by Satan to his eternal ruin. And what can be more just than that they should be taken and charmed with Satan's wiles, who have all their life time rejected and refused to be charmed by the spirit of grace in the scriptures, and sought after the devices of their own hearts? The Lord hath given them up to be fed by the wind of their own inventions, and at last to lie down in sorrow forever. Oh! what shall these venders of the devices and visions of their own heads and hearts do in the great day of God Almighty?

The sixth Remedy is, seriously to consider, that there are no weapons but spiritual weapons sufficiently powerful to withstand the devices of Satan and the arts of false teachers.

EPHESIANS vi. 13.
Wherefore take unto you the whole armor of God,
&c.

You ought to consider that you have not to do with weak and ignorant, but with mighty and subtle enemies; therefore you had need look to it, that your weapons are mighty ; and that they cannot be unless they are spiritual : carnal weapons have no might nor spirit in them towards the making of a conquest upon Satan and his ministers. It was not David's sling nor stone that gave him the honor and advantage of setting his feet upon Goliah, but his faith.

in the name of the Lord of hosts. The only way to stand, conquer, and triumph, is to plead, " 'tis written," as Christ did. There is no sword, but the two-edged sword of the spirit, that will be found to be mettle proof, when the soul comes to engage against Satan: therefore, whenever you contend against Satan and false teachers, always remember to plead, " 'tis written," &c. &c. I would now draw a conclusion by setting before you some special rules, helps, &c. &c.

CONCLUSION.

HELP THE FIRST.

Now if you would not be taken in any of Satan's snares, then be much in prayer.

PSALM cxli. 8, 9, 10.
O God the Lord, in thee is my trust, leave not my soul destitute, &c. &c.

PRAYER is a shelter to the soul, a sacrifice to God, and a scourge to the devil. David's heart was often more out of tune than his harp; he prays, and then, in spite of the devil, cries, " return unto thy rest, O my soul." Prayer is the gate of heaven, a key to let the soul into paradise; there is nothing that renders plots fruitless like prayer. Ah! souls, take you words, and tell God, that Satan hath spread his snares in all places, and in all companies: tell God, that he digs deep, and that he hath plot upon plot, and device upon device, and all to devour you; tell God that you have neither skill nor power to es-

21

cape his wiles: O, tell God that his honor is engaged to stand by you, and to bring you off conquerors: yea, tell your God of the love of Christ, the blood of Christ, and the intercession of Christ; and, finally, tell God of the promised help of the Spirit. Thus shall Satan flee before you.

HELP THE SECOND.

If you would not be overcome through Satan's devices, seek to be filled with the spirit.

EPHESIANS v. 18.
But be filled with the spirit.

Now the spirit of the Lord is a spirit of light and power: and what can the soul do without light and power against spiritual wickedness in high places? 'Tis not enough that you have the spirit, but you must be filled with the spirit, or Satan, that evil spirit, will be too hard for you. Cry for abundance of the spirit: he that supposeth himself to be possessed of enough of the Holy Spirit will quickly find himself vanquished by the evil spirit. Satan hath his snares to take you in prosperity and in adversity, in health and in sickness, in strength and in weakness; when you come to spiritual duties, and when you leave them; in prayer and preaching, in reading and hearing: if you are not filled with the spirit, Satan will be too hard for you, and too crafty for you with all your abilities and experience, and he will frequently lead you captive. Therefore labor more to have your hearts filled with the spirit, than to have your heads filled with notions: so shall you escape the snares of this fowler, and triumph over all his plots and devices practised against your souls.

THE THIRD RULE OR HELP.

If ye would not have Satan to gain any advantage over your souls, then keep a strong, close, and constant watch.

MATTHEW xxvi. 40, 41.
Watch and pray, that ye enter not into temptation.

The soul that will not watch against temptation, must certainly fall before the power of temptation. Satan works most strongly on the fancy when the soul is drowsy. The soul's security is Satan's opportunity to fall upon it, and to spoil it, as Joshua did the men of Ai. The best way to be safe and secure from all the wiles of the devil, is, with Nehemiah and the Jews, to watch and pray, and to pray and watch ; by this means they became too hard for their enemies, and the word of the Lord prospered sweetly in their hands. Remember how Christ chid the sluggishness and negligence of his disciples : " What, could ye not watch with me one hour ?" &c.

Satan will always keep a crafty and malicious watch; shall not Christians, then, keep a holy and spiritual watch? Let us always stand upon our watch-tower, lest we be surprised by this subtle serpent. A watchful soul is a soul upon the wing, a soul out of gun-shot, a soul upon a rock, a soul in a castle, a soul above the clouds, and a soul safe in everlasting arms.

HELP THE FOURTH.

If you would not be taken in any of Satan's devices, then engage not against Satan in your own strength and wisdom.

PHILIPPIANS iv. 13.
I can do all things through Christ, &c.

If we engage against Satan in our own spirits and might, and are strangers to a daily drawing of new virtue and strength from the Lord Jesus Christ, to help in every time of need, we must certainly fall, and that daily. You may see this too evidently before your eyes in every community of professing Christians. The soul that dares to wage war with Satan without new strength and new influence from Jesus, will surely fall before the power of the least temptation. Ah! what a sad instance we find in Peter! Surely he had not looked up to the everlasting hills for strength; but trusting to something in himself he fell into evil. Oh! souls, when ye see the snare, look up to Jesus Christ, and say unto him, "Dear Lord, here is a new plot laid for my soul; give me new wisdom, new strength, new influence, and new measures of grace, that I may escape with honor." Oh! sirs, you must lean more upon Christ than upon duties, and more upon Christ than upon comforts; for without Christ you can do nothing.

HELP THE FIFTH.

If you would not have Satan to prevail against you, then be much in contemplation and longing to be at your heavenly inheritance and home.

PSALM lxxiii. 25.

Whom have I in heaven but thee; and there is none upon earth that I desire besides thee.

Shall the espoused maid long for the marriage-day; the servant for his freedom; the captive for his ransom; the traveler for his inn: the mariner for hi harbor; and the heir for his inheritance? **And** shall not the saints long for the bosom of Christ? There being nothing below his bosom that is not surrounded with Satan's snares. What Paul once said of bonds and afflictions, that they attended him in every place, the same may all the saints say of

21*

Satan's devices, that they attend them in every place; which should cause them to cry out, "Let us go hence, let us go hence:" and say, with Monica, Austin's mother, "What do we here? Why do we not depart hence? Why flee we not swifter?" Let us cry out, with the church of God, "Come, Lord Jesus." Is not Christ the crown of crowns, the glory of glories, and the heaven of heavens? Oh! then, let us still long after a full, clear, and constant enjoyment of Christ in heaven. It is as easy to compass the heavens with a span, and to contain the sea in a nut-shell, as to relate fully Christ's excellencies. "Make haste, my beloved, and be thou like a roe, and come and fetch my soul."

HELP THE SIXTH.

As you would not be taken with any of Satan's devices, then be careful not to grieve the Holy Spirit of God.

EPHESIANS iv. 30.
And grieve not the Holy Spirit of God, whereby ye are sealed, &c.

The divine spirit is very tender, delicate, and jealous of his glory. 'Tis the spirit of the Lord that alone is able to teach us the wiles of the devil, and to point out all his plots, and discover all his secrets ; he, only he can give power and skill to escape those pits that Satan hath digged for your precious souls : but if you grieve and set the sweet and blessed spirit a mourning, by a cold indifference and negligence to his gracious advice and warnings, who can deliver you from falling a prey to the will of your enemy ? Oh ! brethren, be assured, that the spirit will be grieved by your enormities, by your inattention to his gracious voice and comforts, and by giving way to Satan's wiles, until you are ensnared and taken. The spirit of the Lord is your counsellor, your comforter, your upholder, and your strength : 'tis the spirit only that makes a man too great for Satan to conquer. 1 John iv. 4. "Greater is he that is in you than he that is in the world."

DIRECTIONS.

TO THE

MAN THAT GETS TO HEAVEN.

BY JOHN BUNYAN.

———

So run that ye may obtain. 1 Cor. ix. 23.

THESE words are taken from men's running for a wager: A very apt similitude to set before the eyes of the saints of the Lord. "Know you not that they which run in a race run all, but one obtains the prize? So run that ye may obtain." That is, do not only run, but be sure you win as well as run.

The first direction.

If thou wouldst so run as to obtain the kingdom of heaven, then be sure that thou get into the way that leadeth thither; For it is a vain thing to think that ever thou shalt have the prize, though thou runnest never so fast, unless thou art in the way that leads to it. Set the case, that there should be a man

in London that was to run to York for a wager;
now, though he run never so swiftly, yet if he run
full south, he might run himself quickly out of breath,
and be never the nearer the prize, but rather the farther off. Just so it is here; it is not simply the runner, nor yet the hasty runner, that winneth the
crown, unless he be in the way that leadeth thereto.
I have observed, that little time which I have been a
professor, that there is a great running to and fro,
some this way, and some that way, yet it is to be
feared most of them are out of the way, and then,
though they run swift as the eagle can fly, they are
benefited nothing at all.

Here is one runs a quaking, another a ranting;
one again runs after the Baptism, and another after
the Independency; here is one for Free-will, and
another for Presbytery; and yet possibly most of all
these sects run quite the wrong way, and yet every
one is for his life, his soul, either for heaven or hell.

If thou now say, Which is the way? I tell thee
it is CHRIST, THE SON OF MARY, THE
SON OF GOD. Jesus saith, " I am the way, the
truth, and the life; no man cometh to the Father
but by me." So then thy business is, (if thou
wouldst have salvation,) to see if Christ be thine,
with all his benefits, whether he hath covered thee
with his righteousness, whether he hath shewed thee

that thy sins are washed away with his heart blood, whether thou art planted into him, and whether thou have faith in him, so as to make a life out of him, and to confirm thee to him ; that is, such faith as to conclude that thou art righteous, because Christ is thy righteousness, and so constrained to walk with him as the joy of thy heart, because he saved thy soul. And for the Lord's sake take heed, and do not deceive thyself, and think thou art in the way upon too slight grounds ; for if thou miss of the way, thou wilt miss of the prize, and if thou miss of that, I am sure thou wilt lose thy soul, even that soul which is worth more than the whole world.

The second Direction.

As thou shouldest get into the way, so thou shouldest also be much in studying and musing on the way. You know men that would be expert in any thing, they are usually much in studying of that thing, and so likewise is it with those that quickly grow expert in any thing. This therefore thou shouldest do ; let thy study be much exercised about Christ, who is the way ; what he is, what he hath done, and why he is what he is, and why he hath done what is done ; as, why "he took upon him the form of a servant," why he was " made in the likeness of man ;" why he cried ; why he died ; why he " bare the sins of the world ;" why he was made sin, and why he was made righteousness; why he is in heaven in the nature of man, and what he doth there. Be much in musing and considering of these things; be thinking also enough of those which thou must not come near, but leave some on this hand, and some on that hand, as it is with those that travel into other countries, they must leave such a gate on this hand, and such a bush on that hand, and go by such a place, where standeth such a thing. Thus therefore you must do, "Avoid such things which are expressly forbidden in the word of God." "Withdraw thy foot far from her, and come not nigh the door of her house, for her steps take hold of hell, going down to the chambers of death." *And so of every thing that is not in the way*, have a care of it, that thou go not by it; come not near it, have nothing to do with it. So run.

The third Direction.

Not only thus, but in the next place, Thou must strip thyself of those things that may hang upon thee to the hindering of thee in the way to the kingdom of heaven, as covetousness, pride, lust, or whatsoever else thy heart may be inclining unto, which may hinder thee in this heavenly race. Men that run for a wager, if they intend to win as well as run, they do not use to encumber themselves or carry those things about them that may be an hindrance to them in their running. "Every man that striveth for the mastery is temperate in all things:" That is he layeth aside every thing that would be any wise a disadvantage to him; as saith the apostle, "Let us lay aside every weight, and the sin that doth so easily beset us, and let us run with patience the race that is set before us." It is but a vain thing to talk of going to heaven, if thou let thy heart be incumbered with those things that would hinder. Would you not say that such a man would be in danger of losing though he run, if he fills his pocket with stones, hang heavy garments on his shoulders, and great lumpish shoes on his feet? So it is here; thou talkest of going to heaven, and yet fillest thy pocket with stones, i. e. fillest thy heart with this world, lettest that hang on thy shoulders, with its profits and pleasures: Alas, alas, thou art widely mistaken: If thou intendest to win, thou must strip, thou must lay aside every weight, thou must be temperate in all things. Thou must so run.

The fourth Direction.

Beware of by-paths; take heed thou dost not run into those lanes which lead out of the way. There are crooked paths, paths in which men go astray, paths that lead to death and damnation, but take heed of all those. Some of them are dangerous because of practice, some because of opinion, but

22

mind them not: mind the path before thee, look right before thee, turn neither to the right nor to the left, but let thine eyes look right on, even right before thee; "Ponder the path of thy feet, and let all thy ways be established." Turn not to the right hand nor to the left: "Remove thy foot far from evil." This counsel being not so seriously taken as given, is the reason of that starting from opinion to opinion, reeling this way and that way, out of this lane into that lane, and so missing the way to the kingdom. Though the way to heaven be but one, yet there are many crooked lanes and by-paths shoot down upon it, as I may say. And again, notwithstanding the kingdom of heaven be the biggest city, yet usually those by-paths are most beaten, and most travellers go those ways; and therefore the way to heaven is hard to be found, and as hard to be kept in by reason of these.

The fifth Direction.

Do not thou be too much in looking too high in thy journey heavenwards. You know men that run a race do not use to stare and gaze this way and that, neither do they use to cast up their eyes too high, lest haply through their too much gazing with their eyes after other things, they in the mean time stumble and catch a fall. The very same case is this; if thou gaze and stare after every opinion and way that comes into the world, also if thou be prying over much into God's secret decrees, or let thy heart too much entertain questions about some nice foolish curiosities, thou mayest stumble and fall, as many have done, both in ranting and quackery, to their own eternal overthrow, without the marvelous operation of God's grace be suddenly stretched forth to bring them back again. Take heed, therefore, follow not that proud lofty spirit, that, devil-like, cannot be content with his own station. David was of an excellent spirit, where he saith, " Lord, my heart is not haughty, nor mine eyes lofty, neither do I exercise myself in great matters, or things too high for me. Surely I have behaved and quieted myself as a child that is weaned of his mother. My soul is even as a weaned child." Do thou so run.

The sixth Direction.

Take heed that you have not an ear open to every one that calleth after you as you are in your journey. Men that run, you know, if any do call after them, saying, I would speak with you, or go not too fast, and you shall have my company with you, if they run for some great matter, they use to say, alas, I cannot stay, I am in haste, pray talk not to me now; neither can I stay for you, I am running for a wager; if I win I am made, if

I lose I am undone, and therefore hinder me not.—
Thus wise are men when they run for corruptible
things, and thus shouldst thou do, and thou hast
more cause to do so than they, forasmuch as they
run but for things that last not, but thou for an incorruptible glory. I give thee notice of this be-
times, knowing that thou shalt have enough call after thee, even the devil, sin, this world, vain company, pleasure, profits, esteem among men, ease,
pomp, pride, together with an innumerable company of such companions ; one crying, Stay for me :
the other saying, Do not leave me behind ; a third
saying, And take me along with you. What!
will you go, saith the devil, without your sins,
pleasures, and profits ? Are you so hasty ? Can
you not stay and take these along with you ? Will
you leave your friends and companions behind you ?
Can you not do as your neighbors do, carry the world,
sin, lust, pleasure, profit, esteem among men, along
with you ? Have a care thou do not let thine ear
be open to the tempting, enticing, alluring and soul
entangling flatteries of such sink-souls as these are.
" My son, (saith Solomon,) if sinners entice thee,
consent thou not."

The seventh Direction.

In the next place be not daunted though thou
meetest with never so many discouragements in thy
journey thither. That man that is resolved for

heaven, if Satan cannot win him by flatteries, he will endeavor to weaken him by discouragements; saying, thou art a sinner, thou hast broke God's law, thou art not elected, thou comest too late, the day of grace is past, God doth not care for thee, thy heart is naught, thou art lazy, with a hundred other discouraging suggestions. And thus it was with David, where he saith, "I had fainted, unless I had believed to see the loving kindness of the Lord in the land of the living." As if he should say, the devil did so rage and my heart was so base, that had I judged according to my own sense and feeling, I had been absolutely distracted; but I trusted to Christ in the promise, and looked that God would be as good as his promise, in having mercy upon me, an unworthy sinner! and this is that which encouraged me, and kept me from fainting. And thus must thou do when Satan, or the law, or thy own conscience, do go about to dishearten thee, either by the greatness of thy sins, the wickedness of thy heart, the tediousness of the way, the loss of outward enjoyments, the hatred that thou wilt procure from the world, or the like; then thou must encourage thyself with the freeness of the promises, the tender-heartedness of Christ, the merits of his blood, the freeness of his invitations to come in, the greatness of the sin of others that have been pardoned, and that the same God, through the same Christ, holdeth forth the same

grace as free as ever. If these be not thy meditations, thou wilt draw very heavily in the way to
heaven, if thou do not give up all for lost, and
so knock off from following any farther: therefore,
I say, take heart in thy journey, and say to them
that seek thy destruction, "Rejoice not against me,
O my enemy, for when I fall I shall arise, when
I sit in darkness the Lord shall be a light unto
me."

The eighth Direction.

Take heed of being offended at the cross that
thou must go by before thou come to heaven. You
must understand (as I have already touched) that
there is no man that goeth to heaven but he must
go by the cross. The cross is the standing waymark by which all that go to glory must pass by.

"We must through much tribulation enter into
the kingdom of heaven. Yea, and all that will
live godly in Christ Jesus shall suffer persecution."
If thou art in thy way to the kingdom, my life for
thine thou wilt come to the cross shortly, (the Lord
grant that thou shrink not at it, so as to turn back
again.) "If any man will come after me, (saith
Christ,) let him deny himself, and take up his cross
daily, and follow me." The cross it stands, and
hath stood, from the beginning, as a waymark to
the kingdom of heaven. You know if one ask

you the way to such and such a place, you for the
better direction, do not only say, this is the way, but
then also say, you must go by such a gate, by
such a stile, such a bush, tree, bridge, or such
like : Why, so it is here ; thou art inquiring
the way to heaven ? Why, I tell thee, Christ is
the way: into him thou must get, into his righteousness, to be justified ; and if thou art in him,
thou wilt presently see the cross, thou must go close
by it, thou must touch it, nay thou must take it
up, or else thou wilt quickly go out of the way that
leads to heaven, and turn up some of those crooked
lanes that lead down to the chambers of death.

The ninth Direction.

Beg of God that he would do these two things
for thee : First, Enlighten thine understanding :
and secondly inflame thy will. If these two be but
effectually done, there is no fear but thou wilt go
safe to heaven.

One of the great reasons why men and women do
so little regard the other world, it is, because they
see so little of it : And the reason why they see
so little of it is, because they have their understanding darkened : And therefore, saith Paul, " Do
not you believers walk as do other Gentiles, even
in the vanity of their minds, having their under-

standings darkened, being alienated from the life of
God through their ignorance (or foolishness) that
is in them, because of the blindness of their heart."
Walk not as those, run not with them : alas, poor
souls, they have their understandings darkened,
their hearts blinded, and that is the reason they
have such undervaluing thoughts of the Lord Jesus
Christ, and the salvation of their souls.   For when
men do come to see the things of another world,
what a God, what a Christ, what a heaven, and
what an eternal glory there is to be enjoyed: also
when they see that it is possible for them to have a
share in it, I tell you it will make them run
through thick and thin to enjoy it.   Moses having
a sight of this, because his understanding was enlightened, " He feareth not the wrath of the king,
but chose rather to suffer afflictions with the people
of God, than to enjoy the pleasures of sin for a
season."   He refused to be called the son of the
king's daughter; accounting it wonderful riches to
be accounted worthy, of so much as to suffer for
Christ, with the poor despised saints ; and that
was because he saw him who was invisible, and had
respect unto the recompense of reward.   And this
is that which the apostle usually prayeth for in his
epistles for the saints, namely, " That they might
know what is the hope of God's calling, and the
riches of the glory of his inheritance in the saints:
and that they might be able to comprehend with

all saints, what is the breadth and length, and depth
and height, and know the love of Christ, which passeth knowledge." Pray therefore that God would enlighten thy understanding; that will be a very
great help unto thee. It will make thee endure
many a hard brunt for Christ; as Paul saith, " After you were illuminated, ye endured a great fight
of afflictions.——You took joyfully the spoiling
of your goods, knowing in yourselves, that ye have
in heaven a better and an enduring substance." If
there be never such a rare jewel lie just in a man's
way, yet if he sees it not, he will rather trample upon it than stoop for it, and it is because he sees it
not. Why, so it is here, though heaven be worth
never so much, and thou hast never so much need
of it, yet if thou see it not, that is, have not thy
understanding opened or enlightened to see, thou
wilt not regard it at all: therefore cry to the Lord
for enlightening grace, and say, " Lord open my
blind eyes; Lord, take the vail off my dark
heart," shew me the things of the other world, and
let me see the sweetness, glory, and excellency of
them for Christ his sake. This is the first.

The tenth Direction.

Cry to God that he would inflame thy will also
with the things of the other world. For when a
man's will is fully set to do such or such a thing,

then it must be a very hard matter that shall hinder
that man from bringing about his end. When
Paul's will was set resolvedly to go up to Jerusalem, (though it was signified to him before, what
he should there suffer,) he was not daunted at all;
nay, saith he, " I am ready (or willing) not only
to be bound, but also to die at Jerusalem for the
name of the Lord Jesus." His will was inflamed
with love to Christ; and therefore all the persua-
sions that could be used wrought nothing at all.

Your self-willed people nobody knows what to
do with them: we use to say, He will have his own
will, do all what you can. Indeed to have such a
will for heaven is an admirable advantage to a man
that undertaketh a race thither: a man that is resolved, and hath his will fixed, saith he, I will do
my best to advantage myself; I will do my worst
to hinder my enemies; I will not give out as long
as I can stand; I will have it or I will lose my life;
" though he slay me yet will I trust in him." " I
will not let thee go unless thou bless me." I will,
I will, I will, O this blessed inflamed will for heav-
en! What is like it? If a man be willing, then
any argument shall be matter of encouragement;
but if unwilling, then any argument shall give dis-
couragement; this is seen both in saints and sinners: in them that are the children of God, and also those that are the children of the devil. As,

1. The saints of old, they were willing and resolved for heaven, what could stop them? Could
fire and faggot, sword or halter, filthy dungeons,
whips, bears, bulls, lions, cruel rackings, stoning,
starving, nakedness, &c. " And in all these things
they were more than conquerors, through him
that loved them;" who had also made them " willing
in the day of his power."

2. See again, on the other side, the children of
the devil, because they are not willing, how many
shift and starting holes they will have. I have married a wife, I have a farm, I shall offend my land-
lord, I shall offend my master, I shall lose my tra-
ding, I shall lose my pride, my pleasures, I shall
be mocked, and scoffed, therefore I dare not come.
I, saith another, will stay till I am older, till my
children are out, till I get a little aforehand in the
world, till I have done this and that, and the other
business; but alas, the thing is, they are not
willing; for, were they but soundly willing, these,
and a thousand such as these, would hold them no
faster than the cords held Sampson, when he broke
them like burnt flax. I tell you the will is all: that
is, one of the chief things which turns the wheel
either backwards or forwards; and God knoweth
that full well, and so likewise doth the devil; and
therefore they both endeavor very much to strengthen
the will of their servants; God, he is for making

of his a willing people to serve him; and the devil
he doeth what he can to possess the will and affection of those that are in love to sin; and therefore
when Christ comes close to the matter, indeed, saith
he, "You will not come to me." "How often
would I have gathered you as a hen doth her chick-
ens, but you would not." The devil had possessed
their wills, and so long he was sure enough of them.
O therefore cry hard to God to inflame thy will
for heaven and Christ: thy will, I say, if that be
rightly set for heaven, thou wilt not be beat off with
discouragements; and this was the reason that when
Jacob wrestled with the angel, though he lost a
limb as it were, and the hollow of his thigh was
put out of joint as he wrestled with him, yet saith
he, "I will not," mark, "I will not let thee go
except thou bless me." Get thy will tipt with the
heavenly grace, and resolution against all discouragements, and then thou goest full speed for heaven;
but if thou faulter in thy will, and be not found
there, thou wilt run hobbling and halting all the way
thou runnest, and also thou wilt be sure to fall short
at last. The Lord give thee a will and courage.